business *masterminds*

bill
GATES

ROBERT HELLER

A Dorling Kindersley Book

www.dk.com

Dorling Kindersley

LONDON, NEW YORK, DELHI, JOHANNESBURG,
MUNICH, PARIS and SYDNEY

DK www.dk.com

Senior Editor Adèle Hayward
US Editor Gary Werner
Senior Art Editor Caroline Marklew
Project Art Editors Christine Lacey,
Laura Watson
DTP Designer Jason Little
Production Controller Elizabeth Cherry
Managing Editor Stephanie Jackson
Managing Art Editor Nigel Duffield

Produced for Dorling Kindersley by
Grant Laing Partnership 48 Brockwell
Park Gardens, London SE24 9BJ
Managing Editor Jane Laing
Project Editor Helen Ridge
Managing Art Editor Steve Wilson

Published in the United States by
Dorling Kindersley Publishing, Inc.
95 Madison Avenue
New York, New York 10016

First American Edition, 2000
2 4 6 8 10 9 7 5 3 1

**Library of Congress Cataloging-in-
Publication Data**

Heller, Robert, 1932-
Bill Gates / Robert Heller.
p. cm. – (Business masterminds)
Includes bibliographical references and
index.
ISBN 0-7894-5159-X (acid-free paper)
1. Gates, Bill, 1955-
2. Businessmen. I. Title.

HD9696.63.U62 G37444 2000
338.7'610053'092–dc21   99-056434

Reproduced by Colourpath, London
Printed in Hong Kong by Wing King Tong

Author's Acknowledgments
The many sources for this book have been
acknowledged in the text, but I must now
express my great debt to everybody, above
all to the Mastermind himself. Nor would
the book exist but for the inspiration and
effort of the excellent Dorling Kindersley
team – to whom my warm thanks.

Packager's Acknowledgments
Grant Laing Partnership would like to
thank the following for their help and
participation:
Editorial Lee Stacy, Frank Ritter;
Design Sarah Williams;
Index Kay Ollerenshaw.

Publisher's Acknowledgments
Dorling Kindersley would like to thank the
following for their help and participation:
Editorial Josephine Bryan, Claire Ellerton,
Nicola Munro, Jane Simmonds;
Design Austin Barlow, Tracy Hambleton-
Miles, Nigel Morris; Laura Watson;
DTP Rob Campbell, Louise Waller;
Picture research Andy Sansom.

Contents

Master of the information age

Without Bill Gates, the personal computer would still have conquered the world. He triumphed at Microsoft by arriving on the threshold of the new era, combining widely known technology with practical application of extraordinarily powerful business ideas. Gates is a master of software technology, but no technological genius; he is a brilliant manager who has found inspiration even in crisis.

That ability was severely tested when the spread of PCs to homes accompanied and accelerated the sensational rise of the Internet. Gates's late but powerful response culminated in his 1999 book, *Business @ the Speed of Thought*, in which he donned the mantle of prophet of the revolution. That revolution, though, has taken his company into a new and problematical era.

The Internet challenges the strengths of Microsoft as never before. Meeting the challenge of change, though, is crucial to Gates's pragmatic approach to realizing powerful visions. He has been a spokesman for change, whose actions have spoken louder than words in making him both prime mover and chief figurehead of the Age of Information.

Robert Heller

Biography

William Henry Gates III was born in 1955 to a well-to-do, well-connected Seattle family, which sent him to Harvard to study law (his father's profession). His story is not that of poor boy made good. The saga of Microsoft, however, is typical of the electronics industry – tiny, poor company made great and rich. Gates went to a private school, where he excelled at mathematics, and became fascinated from his early teens by personal computing, then in its formative stage.

With an equally enthusiastic Seattle friend, Paul Allen, Gates wrote a version of the BASIC computer language in 1975 for an early PC, the MITS Altair. Immediately following this success Gates and Allen formed Microsoft (initially Micro-Soft), and, in 1977, Gates abandoned college to concentrate on the new industry. The breakthrough for the pair came in 1980 when two IBM executives visited Microsoft to commission work on BASIC for their new PC – a rush program with unprecedentedly tight deadlines.

The IBM-ers found an engaging, bespectacled, highly intelligent and articulate man, physically restless and with great mental agility. Gates has not changed since. He reads voluminously, even in odd moments, specializes in "multi-tasking" (doing many things at once), and somehow contrives to give the running of Microsoft his full attention, while also spending much time on public relations. He appears to have no outside interests other than his family, his Porsches and his magnificent, technology-crammed lakeside mansion in Medini, Washington. His investments outside Microsoft alone are worth $11.5 billion. His Microsoft shares are worth seven times that stupendous sum.

Creating the industry standard

All this wealth sprang, not from work on BASIC, but from IBM's other need, for operating software for their PC. Gates boldly bid for the contract. He then approached another software company – Seattle Computer Products – and bought an operating system called Q-DOS (nicknamed Quick and Dirty Operating System). Gates and Allen then modified it to suit IBM's needs, renamed it MS-DOS (Microsoft Disk Operating System) and delivered it to IBM for a relatively low price, undercutting rival software companies. Gates's purchase of Q-DOS for only $50,000 opened the doors to billions, largely because IBM, grossly underestimating the market for its PC, signed a contract allowing Microsoft to sell the software to any other PC manufacturer. When the PC took off, astounding IBM executives by its success, Microsoft's wealthy future was assured – to the rising annoyance of IBM.

The constant threat to Gates, even as his sales and profits grew astronomically with the rise of the IBM and IBM-compatible PCs, was that IBM would break the vital link with MS-DOS. Gates protected Microsoft as best he could by partnering IBM in the development of a new operating system, OS/2. When IBM executives sought to dissolve the OS/2 partnership, Gates won a reprieve at a June 1986 lunch with CEO John Akers.

Capturing the PC market

Little more than three years later, the war between IBM and Microsoft broke into the open. In 1990, Gates won hands down with the launch of Windows 3.0. Using the same technique – the "graphical user interface" – that had made the Apple Macintosh so popular, with its graphic icons and pull-down menus, the new product was selling a million copies a month by 1993. It gave users vastly improved access to applications, opening another door of opportunity for Gates. Now Microsoft could write and sell a whole new line of application programs for use with Windows.

Products like Word, the word processing program, and the Excel spreadsheet, are almost as dominant as MS-DOS and Windows, which hold 90 percent of the operating system market for PCs. Gates kept piling on the pressure. Windows NT, a more powerful product aimed at the corporate market, appeared in 1993. Like the first version of Windows, NT had serious defects. But Gates's approach has always been to launch first and improve later, radically if need be.

What worked so well with Windows 3.0 also triumphed with NT. Microsoft's sales and staff numbers soared, and up went the profits and the share price. Each advance in the stock made a new millionaire among the Microsoft ranks. But all the employee nesteggs were spectacularly outweighed by the fabulous fortune created for Gates himself. His reputation as a technological genius (undeserved) and as a superb businessman (definitely merited) was eclipsed by his unquestionable standing as The World's Richest Man.

The challenge of the Internet

Whether or not the adulation and success temporarily blunted Gates's vision, the company, having beaten IBM so decisively, nearly defeated itself by failing to react to the early, obvious challenge of the Internet. Since operating systems and applications could be loaded from cyberspace, Microsoft's hegemony could be undermined, like IBM's before it. By May 1995, Gates had become fully aware of the threat: one of the countless memos he regularly

Environmentally friendly futuristic house
Gates's Lake Washington estate was still under construction when the family moved in during 1998. Built from reclaimed Douglas fir timber, the 40,000 sq. ft. mansion is computer-controlled inside.

emails to "Microsofties" (as employees at Microsoft are known) was called "The Internet Tidal Wave." It gave the new technology "the highest level of importance."

Billions of dollars of development capital were switched to the assault on the new market – and especially on Netscape, the company whose Internet browsers, initially given away free, had taken it from an April 1994 start-up to $5 billion of market capitalization by December the next year. Gates had an immensely powerful weapon to deploy. The technique was to compel PC manufacturers to pre-load the Microsoft browser on to their machines as an allegedly integral part of Windows 95, the popular replacement for Windows 3.0.

Although commercially successful, the onslaught on Netscape made Microsoft vulnerable legally. In 1998 the US government's antitrust action went to trial, producing months of high embarrassment – and a hostile verdict – for Gates and the company. Now married to a former Microsoft employee – Melinda French – and with two children, Gates has arrived at a crossroads. Will the industry he has done more than anybody to create move away from his control? Can he reverse the growing tide of unfavorable opinion?

Unpopular figure

Public sentiment had run against Gates because of his very success. Some may have simply envied his enormous fortune, or resented that the multi-billionaire was not spreading his wealth as generously as he could afford. Within the computer industry, Microsoft's power to crush competitors, and to dominate its terms of trade with the PC manufacturers, aroused more than envy. Firms were anxious about their own profits and prospects as Microsoft extended the range of its products and its ambitions. As for the PC buyers, they typically accepted the Microsoft software bundled in with their purchases as a fact of life.

Many of the "techies," however, felt that Gates was a restrictive and too powerful force, whose hold over the technology prevented important advances and trapped users into costly upgrades to a system that was inherently old-fashioned. This mood led to an open hostility that expressed itself in many ways, ranging from Internet attacks to published books, such as *Barbarians Led by Bill Gates: Microsoft from the Inside*. A "cookbook" gave the recipe for "Breaking Bill Gates's Windows Monopoly (without Breaking Windows) with Linux CD Operating

System." This title referred to a new system, available either free over the Internet, or from intermediaries who charged vastly less than Microsoft did for its own system.

Fighting the antitrust action

Linux was seized upon by "techies" as the answer to their anti-Gates prayers. A significant number of corporate users also adopted Linux (which has important advantages over the Microsoft system). This gave Gates another weapon in his battle against the antitrust authorities. He argued that Microsoft cannot be described as a monopoly when competition is more intense than ever and when customers are gaining from falling prices and greater performance. Unfortunately, this defense was not helped by taped interviews with Gates, screened at the Washington trial. Along with other evidence (such as internal e-mails), the tapes showed Gates in an unflattering and sometimes apparently evasive light.

As a consequence of the antitrust trial, Gates had been forced into the public arena as never before. After a hesitant reaction, he responded with his usual determination. TV interviews showed a relaxed, smiling man, with no hint of defensiveness. Moreover, Gates and his wife decided to set up a gigantic charitable foundation to control and distribute the bulk of their wealth: they could hope (like the Rockefellers before them) to swing public opinion in their favor. Gates also pushed through a major reorganization of Microsoft to delegate more of his power, while continuing to direct its huge switch of strategy to the Internet. And on one issue he remains quite determined: to carry on doing the job he loves in an industry which, more than any other man, he has so long commanded.

1

IT changes absolutely everything

Creating a universal space for information sharing, collaboration, and commerce ● **Interaction between the firm's "Web workstyle" and customers' "Web lifestyle"** ● Why the Internet's universal connection produces a true customer-centric world ● **How the Internet enables the vital "digital nervous system" (DNS)** ● Management changes that flow from the economic impact of cyberspace ● **Restructuring processes are more fundamental than any change since mass production**

Bill Gates's philosophy and success are inseparable from the Information Revolution. From the start he wanted to create "a tool for the Information Age that could magnify your brainpower instead of just your muscle power." He sees digital tools as the means of augmenting the unique powers of the human being: thinking, articulating thought, working together with other humans to act on thought. In management terms, his success has been built on the proposition that information technology must and will change everything – including the ways in which companies communicate, are managed, win competitive advantage, and do business.

After years devoted to advocating and enabling a revolution centering on the personal computer, his objective shifted in the mid-1990s to positioning Microsoft at the head of a new revolution founded on the Internet, which, he says, "is still at the beginning."

Underestimating the Internet

The Internet's central position in Gates's thought and action represents a great personal turnround. When the first Website appeared in 1993, to be followed shortly by Netscape's Internet browser, Gates could hardly fail to notice these events. But, as he has often admitted, he was slow to understand the fundamental significance of Internet developments. Appearing at a *Fortune* lecture in 1998 with the fabled investor Warren Buffett, Gates confessed that "when the Internet came along, we had it as fifth or sixth priority."

He told himself, "Yeah, I've got that on my list, so I'm okay." This was far from the truth. "There came a point when we realized it was happening faster and was a much deeper phenomenon than had been recognized in our strategy," he recalled. His realization was prompted, not by intellectual arousal, but by commercial necessity. Well before Gates woke up, many commentators had identified the Internet as a major threat to Microsoft's quasi-monopoly.

Entering the Web race

The time lag is especially astonishing in the light of Gates's own later views. By 1999, he saw the Internet as far more than a priority. It had become, in his mind and in actuality, a transcendent technology. "The Internet creates a new universal space for information sharing, collaboration, and commerce," wrote Gates in *Business @ the Speed of Thought* (1999). This "new medium" combines the functionalities of television and telephone with those of paper in a way that reshapes all relationships. As Gates observed, "the ability to find information and match people with common interests is completely new."

A clue to understanding Gates's initial failure to grasp the overwhelming importance of the Internet lies in an earlier lapse. In 1981 Gates affirmed, when forecasting the future of personal computers, that "640k ought to be enough for anybody." Today, when desktops routinely have 128MB of memory and six gigabytes of hard drive space, that prediction sounds ludicrous. But Gates's commercial

"We didn't see that the Internet, a network for academics and techies, would blossom into the global commercial network it is today."
Business @ the Speed of Thought

interests then seemed best served by stable development of PC power, rather than its headlong expansion. His erroneous thinking was wishful. His complacency regarding an Internet that threatened to bypass his quasi-monopoly of PC software was just as wishful.

By 1998 Gates saw clearly that the emerging hardware, software, and communication standards "will reshape business and consumer behavior." In fact, the "will" reads oddly, since that reshaping is already taking place on a broad front and a large scale. Most of the functions Gates offered as predictions were being widely applied even as he wrote. People "will regularly use PCs at work and at home," he asserted; they already do. They also already "use email routinely," and they are connected to the Internet by the millions. Many also carry digital devices containing their personal and business information.

Pocket-sized information
An enormous storage capacity coupled with a light, compact design makes the digital personal organizer ideal for keeping track of appointments, addresses, and important dates.

Changing workstyle and lifestyle

It takes no great prophetic leap to see that these digital tools, already employed by many people, will spread to the great majority, even without the new consumer devices such as television set-top boxes that Gates confidently and rightly expects. Gates fits current and impending developments into two important constructs: "Web workstyle" and "Web lifestyle." Neither had been fully realized by 1999, but their shape was clear. "Web workstyle" springs from the use of digital methods to change business processes. "Web lifestyle" changes the nature of the relationship between consumers and the businesses that serve them.

Web workstyle and Web lifestyle obviously interact. Changed corporate processes are essential to meet the demands of customers who want to transact their business online. At present, corporations can still treat Web transactions as ancillary, since they represent only a tiny proportion of all trade; but Gates predicts that this will not always be the case. He believes strongly in a concept popularized by his friend Andy Grove, the CEO of Intel. The microprocessor leader stresses the importance of "inflection points," at which the technology generates "sudden and massive" change.

Gates predicts that this kind of change is what will happen when Internet connections leave the desktop and become portable, when "everyday devices such as water and electrical meters, security systems, and automobiles will be connected... reporting on their usage and status." The connection will be with the same portable devices that "will keep us constantly in touch with other systems and other people." The combined results will transform lifestyles and business styles alike.

Reshaping the way we live

Gates points out that earlier technologies entirely reshaped the way people lived. The convincing example that he cites is electricity. Until its infrastructure had become available, people had no idea of the powerful electrical devices, from telephones to television, that would change the world. The essence of the Internet is electronic applications. These have multiplied and are multiplying so fast that the "adoption of technology for the Web lifestyle is happening faster than the adoption of electricity, cars, television, and radio."

The practical results of this on-rushing technological revolution are clearly imminent. Even in 1998, only a tiny percentage of transactions in the US, let alone worldwide, were transacted on the Internet. Gates cites the fact that "only about one million of the 15 billion total bills in the United States were paid electronically." The growth rate, however, is so phenomenal – with Web use doubling every 100 days – that it is easy for him to predict a future in which digital transactions will not only be universal, but greatly enriched in functionality.

Each customer will have a personal banking page on the Web from which all transactions can be conducted and all financial information obtained. This is not a vision, but an extrapolation of irreversible trends. Gates is on the safest possible ground in predicting that one year into the millennium more than 60 percent of US households will have PCs and 85 percent of these will have Internet access. Drawing from his experience in the PC era, Gates believes in the unstoppable advance of the technology and the consequent profusion of popular applications.

The impact on lifestyle begins with television. "Over time the biggest impact of digital television will be the ability to integrate other digital data, providing interactivity, smart agents [software programs that act as pickers and choosers on your behalf], targeted advertising and sales offers, and access to the Web." Gates is fully conscious that technical obstacles still exist to ensuring "a simple and totally digital television experience for viewers." Difficulties include common standards and bandwidth, "the information carrying capacity of a digital communications system." But, as ever, he has confidence in technology's powers to remove the obstacles: "the advances on many fronts make it likely that the speed of improvement will surprise everyone in the next decade."

Bringing people together

Looking at the "enormous" social implications of the Web lifestyle and workstyle, Gates concludes that the Internet will bring people together rather than causing "society to fly apart." He sees its main product as universal communication, which broadens rather than narrows horizons. The "communities" that people began to build early in Internet history, in which groups with common interests joined together, are a new and powerful means of bonding. "The Web lets you join communities across the globe and provides the opportunity to strengthen connections in your own backyard," writes Gates.

People will win time for these new social interactions from the enhanced efficiency of Web transactions. Gates does not believe that the Web lifestyle will generate changes in human nature or fundamental ways of life, although he gives no evidence for this conclusion. Rather, he sees people following much the same interests, but "in a better way." For example, the Web brings shopping into the home, both in the selection of products and services and in their delivery, and offers infinite choice and variety. As Gates observes, this produces "a true customer-centric world."

Developing a DNS

Gates, however, devotes much more attention to the business transformation, the contours of which are clearly visible, than to the more opaque consumer world. The key digital applications for business include:

- Replacing paperwork with digital text
- Facilitating groupwork by enabling teams to use the same data simultaneously
- Providing up-to-the-minute information about sales and customers to improve responsiveness
- Facilitating relationships with business partners

Microsoft itself is used and cited as a test-bed for these applications. Gates makes large claims for the "new level of electronic intelligence" that has been infused into his company. His metaphor is the "biological nervous system that triggers your reflexes so that you can react quickly to danger or need." A "digital nervous system," or DNS, is the business equivalent. It consists of "the digital processes that enable a company to perceive and react to its environment, to sense competitor challenges and customer needs, and to organize timely responses."

Before his Internet conversion, Gates believed that the future lay with networking PCs, joining them together within organizations. He now describes this technology as "a mere network of computers" compared to a DNS, which combines hardware and software to provide "accuracy, immediacy, and richness" of information with "the insight and collaboration made possible by the information." The distinction is partly semantic, but it is correct that the sheer universality of the Internet, which is crucial to a DNS, is truly revolutionary in its consequences.

Changing how companies work

Companies are having to develop a digital nervous system in order to keep pace with markets in which "consumers are demanding faster service, stronger relationships, and personalization." Consequently, adopting the Web workstyle is not an option for management but a necessity. For businesses of all sizes, this certainly does mean fundamental changes in the way they are organized and how they work. In turn, these changes cannot take place without profound socioeconomic results, since people depend on businesses for their work, livelihoods, many relationships, and the supply of goods and services.

Gates accurately delineates the fundamental management changes engendered by the Internet's economic impact. The effects will be great and will spread far beyond companies. Many companies are already moving in the directions he describes:

- Focusing on their "core competencies" and outsourcing everything else to outside suppliers
- Maintaining a small central core of people, and employing others as and when required
- Expanding rapidly and even globally from small or medium-sized bases
- Escaping from geographic constraints by transferring work to where it is best and/or most economically done

- Refocusing all processes on the customer, and constantly mutating to meet changing markets and competition
- Increasing the pressure to shorten cycle time and increase the speed of all other processes

As for the consequences, they are already appearing. Secure full-time employment with companies is dropping away markedly and less secure, part-time, freelance employment is rising. Established companies have to counter increasing threats from many new competitors,

Working from home
The rise in the amount of work that is outsourced is bringing increased flexibility to the lives of many, making it easier to fulfill the demands of both work and family.

with size and geographical spread no longer the defensive bastions that they were in the past. Many jobs that have been available in the mature economies are being exported. Specialization is increasing markedly as the key beneficiaries of "outsourcing" concentrate and coalesce. Prices are falling as processes become faster and cheaper.

Gates observes that "almost all the time involved in producing an item is in the coordination of the work, not in the actual production.... Good information systems can remove most of that waiting time.... The speed of delivery and the interaction with the Internet effectively shifts products into services." It follows that the Internet turns each and every product company around by 180 degrees – from production first to customer first. The corporate cultures and infrastructures must "support fast research, analysis, collaboration, and execution" – which currently is far from reality.

Restructuring business processes

Perhaps influenced by Microsoft's own characteristics, which much more nearly reflect the needs of the digital revolution, Gates does not dwell on the upheavals (including the job losses) that will result as business leaders "streamline and modernize their processes and their organization" in the effort to "get the full benefit of technology." He argues strongly for these reforms, because giving people responsibility and authority without information leaves them "helpless." Moreover, a business loses a "huge advantage" by not moving into the Internet mode.

In this mode "information about production systems, product problems, customer crises and opportunities, sales shortfalls, and other important business news gets through the organization in a matter of minutes instead of days." The "right people," too, are "working on the issues within hours." Gates regards this restructuring of processes as "more fundamental than any other change since mass production." If this is correct, though, it surely invalidates his next statement: "every company can choose whether to lead or follow the emerging digital trends."

Embracing constant change

This option must have disappeared in what Gates describes as a time of "industry-wrenching change." He distinguishes the current era from previous economic epochs by stressing that industries used to be wrenched around for short periods, interspersed by long periods of stability. The evolutionary term for this is "punctuated equilibrium." The Age of the Internet, on the other hand, features an environment of constant change, or "punctuated chaos."

Gates uses financial crises – such as the one which raged in Asia in 1998 – as a metaphor for this condition. Already, all financial players are digitally connected, so "any downturn or upturn in a major market creates overnight reverberations in other markets." The wired world is a world in constant flux in which "digital interconnections will soon exist for all markets." The problem, though, is also the solution. "The digital world is both forcing companies to react to change and giving them the tools by which to stay ahead of it." IT provides the quick reflexes that connect business strategy with organizational response. Without IT, there will be no response – and presumably no company.

Gates puts this choice succinctly: "it's evolve rapidly or die." He sees no downside to the digital age. True, he sees that there are important political and social dimensions.

But the Internet issues he raises, which "include how we ensure access for everyone and how we protect children," are only subsets of the broader question: how to "ensure that the new digital age reflects the society" that citizens want to create. In his view, what they want is what they are getting. Gates sees only universal benefit: improved products and services, more responsiveness to complaints, lower costs and more choices, better government, and more economical social services.

Ideas into action

- Form teams able to use the same data simultaneously.

- Combine hardware and software for accuracy, immediacy, and richness of information.

- Meet customer demands for faster service, stronger relationships, and personalization.

- Focus on "core competencies" and outsource everything else to outsiders.

- Coordinate work to radically reduce time spent on production.

- Streamline and modernize to get the full benefit of technology.

- Choose right now to follow the emerging digital trends.

The opening of windows to the world

The early years and final triumph of Microsoft can only be understood in the context of the mighty IBM, with its massive market share, huge spending on technology, and stranglehold on large corporate customers.

Compared to IBM, for all its own success, Microsoft was a midget for its first decade. For that reason, Gates centered his strategy around IBM during this time. He needed to keep the corporation's business, because the colossus dominated the market.

But Gates also wanted to realize his vision of universal personal computing. That meant cheaper computers, widely distributed, and working to a common standard, enabling anybody to use any program on any computer. His vision was incompatible with IBM's strongest motivation, which was to sustain its sales of high-priced computers to high-spending corporates and to sell proprietary systems that could only be used by purchasers of IBM machines.

Its drive for exclusivity gave IBM a powerful motive for removing Microsoft from its path. This was impossible, however, as long as every PC sold by IBM used MS-DOS as its operating system. The strategy that evolved in 1984–87 was simple, although it required billions in investment: devise a new operating system, which would markedly improve on the "clunky" MS-DOS, and link the system to a new line of PCs that would blow the IBM "clones," all using Microsoft products, out of the water.

Dual strategy

Gates would have been destroyed in that explosion. To protect Microsoft, he pursued a dual strategy. First, hang in there with IBM at all costs, working with the company on the new system – OS/2. Second, build on MS-DOS to improve its performance and increase its attractions to software writers and customers, primarily by adding graphical capability.

If the "new" MS-DOS – which came to be called Windows – was sufficiently attractive, then IBM would be obliged to offer the system. Microsoft could retain its existing markets and build on the new technology base to broaden

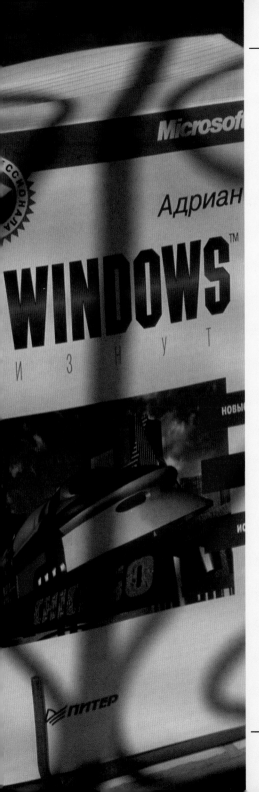

> **"We'd lost the chance to make Windows and OS/2 compatible, and because we'd lost the struggle to make the OS/2 run on modest machines, it only made sense to continue to develop Windows."**
> *The Road Ahead*

and strengthen its own line of highly profitable applications.

The obvious drawback to this dual strategy was that Gates needed IBM more than IBM needed Microsoft. This was equally obvious to the IBMers, many of whom resented the fame and fortune that Gates had won through his brilliant contract with their company. While Gates resisted attempts to shut him out (even offering IBM up to 30 percent of Microsoft, and being turned down), cooperation on OS/2 went badly. "I felt that the OS/2 project would be a ticket to the future for both companies," he commented. "Instead, it eventually created an enormous rift between us."

Gates lists the failure among his greatest mistakes; but in truth the dual strategy worked fabulously to his advantage. As OS/2 failed in the marketplace, Windows took off to become the world's most successful software product. For Microsoft, Windows was not so much a ticket to the future as a golden passport.

2

Building a knowledge company

Mastering the five disciplines that make the learning organization work ● **Why employee success depends more on good hiring than subsequent experienc**● Developing a high corporate IQ by exchanging information widely ● **The need to make sharing an integral part o work** ● Using hands-on management to evangelize, recognize, reward, and review information usage ● **Four ways in which bosses must raise the corporate IQ ●**

Microsoft has been credited with being a genuine example of the "learning organization." This is not a phrase used by Bill Gates, perhaps because of its vagueness. As a hard-nosed businessman, Gates is only interested in concrete results. The key to the learning organization is "knowledge management." Even in the second edition of *The Road Ahead*, published in 1996, there is little sign of this theme. But his thinking has undergone considerable change since then, and by 1999 knowledge management loomed very large in Gates's outlook. It is central to the philosophy he expressed in that year's book – *Business @ the Speed of Thought*.

Does Microsoft in fact practice what its master preaches? The company's principles and processes do embrace the five "learning disciplines" identified by Peter Senge – a professor at Massachusetts Institute of Technology and author of *The Fifth Discipline* (1990). These disciplines are described as the basis of "learning organization work." They are:

Personal Mastery. Expecting people to develop their personal capacity to meet their own objectives, and thus those of the company, which in turn is organized to encourage that personal effort

Mental Models. Developing the right "mind-set" to guide actions and decisions

Shared Vision. Commitment of all members of the organization to its aims and its ways of achieving those objectives

Team Learning. Exploiting the fact that group thinking is greater than the sum of its individual parts

Increasing the "bandwidth"

These five disciplines also fit the picture which Randall E. Stross paints, in *The Microsoft Way* (1996), of Bill Gates as a "practical intellectual." In the software industry, this is not a contradiction in terms. It requires genuine intellect to write software, but the software is useless unless it works in practice. Narrow-minded technologists have never fitted Gates's broader ambitions. He is famous for using the word "bandwidth" to describe people's intellectual capacity: it is a metaphor drawn from the amount of information that a communications system can carry.

Gates believes that the greater the human "bandwidth" that he employs (in other words, the more collective intelligence Microsoft hires), the greater the strength of his company. He is less interested in the amorphous concept of a "learning organization" than in the harder notion of a "knowledge company," which stores and develops its intellectual resources, and augments them by its hiring policies. The knowledge company's raw material is brainpower. You hire the best and best-trained brains, create an environment in which they can create their best work, and build systems so that the knowledge that has been created is built into the fabric and operations of the business – where it can be shared and transmitted.

Hiring the super smart

The brightest and best of the new university graduates who approach the company (of whom only a small minority are hired) are invited to enter the Microsoft campus. The headquarters site in Redmond, Washington, has been described as "organized along the lines of a university." Gates seeks not just the smart, but the "super smart." According to Stross, the super smart have every one of the following attributes:

- Ability to grasp new knowledge very fast
- Ability to pose acute questions instantaneously
- Perception of connections between different areas of knowledge
- At-a-glance "linguistic" ability to interpret software code
- Obsessive concern with the problem on hand, even when away from work
- Great powers of concentration
- Photographic recall of their work

All of these attributes, including the amazing recall, are personal characteristics of Gates himself. He expects them to be accompanied by an emphasis on pragmatism, verbal agility, and swift response to challenge – qualities that also reflect Gates's own aptitudes. He believes that he was born, not made, and that the success of an employee at Microsoft

Campus environment
Microsoft headquarters in Redmond, Washington, has the appearance and atmosphere of a university campus, encouraging creativity and intellectual pursuits in the graduate employees.

depends more on the hiring than on the subsequent experience. That would explain why, to quote Stross:

> "... the best programmers are not marginally better than merely good ones. They are an order of magnitude better, measured by whatever standard: conceptual creativity, speed, ingenuity of design, or problem-solving ability. All else being equal, the company that recruits the largest number of... the alphas among alphas is most likely to win the biggest sweepstakes."

Deploying the best brains

This theory raises a practical problem. Although Gates has indeed won the biggest prizes, the company's history has been marred by conspicuous technical failures, such as the persistent clumsiness of MS/DOS, problems with the early versions of Windows, the almost fatal flop of Windows NT, and misfires with several applications. Clearly, hiring the best brains is not enough. How they are deployed and organized is decisive in the effectiveness of their output. This is where the knowledge company, as opposed to the learning organization, makes its mark.

Here, too, the hard head of Gates the businessman is at variance with the philosopher of mental bandwidth. For all the "campus" elements, Microsoft is no university but a hard-driving commercial enterprise, which, sometimes counterproductively, is only interested in hard results. In an effort to control costs, Microsoft has always deliberately sought to hire fewer people than it actually needs, following the formula "n minus one," where n equals the numbers required. While excessive headcount is to be deplored, inadequate numbers also exert a harmful effect: overwork and over-stretching carry obvious risks.

Sharing knowledge

Gates himself is clear that high individual intelligence is not enough "in today's dynamic markets." A company also needs a high corporate IQ, which hinges on the facility to share information widely and enable staff members "to build on each other's ideas." This is partly a matter of storing the past, partly of exchanging current knowledge. As individuals learn, their knowledge adds to the corporate store.

What matters most is quality, not quantity; how effectively that store is mobilized by collaborative working. "The ultimate goal is to have a team develop the best ideas from throughout an organization and then act with the same unity of purpose and focus that a single, well-motivated person would bring to bear on a situation," says Gates. That way, the super-smart, articulate person – the Bill Gates archetype – becomes the organization writ large. It is the boss's role to encourage collaboration and knowledge sharing, using not just exhortation but reward for the purpose.

Gates advocates setting up specific projects that share knowledge across the organization and making this sharing "an integral part of the work itself – not an add-on frill." Rejecting the old adage that "knowledge is power," Gates argues that "power comes not from knowledge kept, but from knowledge shared" – and managed.

"We read, ask questions, explore, go to lectures, compare notes and findings... consult experts, daydream, brainstorm, formulate and test hypotheses, build models and simulations, communicate what we're learning, and practice new skills." *The Road Ahead*

Managing knowledge effectively

On this reading, knowledge management must be of extreme importance. Yet Gates seems to downplay it when he writes: "Knowledge management is a fancy term for a simple idea. You're managing data, documents, and people's efforts." He goes on to explain at great length how these three processes can be deployed in the following four areas of any business:

- Planning
- Customer service
- Training
- Project collaboration

Some of the applications – for instance, in training and customer service – are not especially high-level, but they plainly serve essential purposes and answer important questions. What happens, for example, if Microsoft salespeople out in the field get queries from customers? The sales force cannot be expected to have the technical knowledge that resides in the product groups. By operating through a Website called the InfoDesk, Microsoft's product people can answer 90 percent of all questions within two days. Company-wide access to product knowledge is a crucial aspect of the corporate IQ.

Access to training is also critical and has an obvious relationship to the effectiveness of corporate brainpower. Again, the needs can be met with high efficiency online. Microsoft employees can find the course they want, get notified when it is available, and register through a single site. In addition, the Web can provide not only training information but the training itself (using multimedia and chat sites, for example). During 1998 online facilities at

Microsoft trained twice as many students as went on physical courses. Gates regards this as fundamental management of knowledge – which it clearly is.

Creating a collaborative culture

What excites him more, however, is creating a "collaborative culture, reinforced by information flow [which] makes it possible for smart people all over a company to be in touch with one another." The technology again plays a crucial role, helping to stimulate and energize the workplace. That happens as a "critical mass of high-IQ people," working in concert, share a vital experience, and

Stimulating atmosphere
By encouraging members of staff to work together and exchange ideas, Gates looks for a highly motivated and enthusiastic workforce happy to work long hours to achieve specified goals.

"the energy level shoots way up." Gates believes that cross-stimulation breeds new ideas, raises the contribution levels of the less experienced employees, and gets the whole company working "smarter."

That does not happen by itself. Effective knowledge management is both a means and an end. Every time an internal Microsoft consultant finishes an assignment, he or she is required to send technology solutions to a central Web location called InSite. But digital technology is not the whole answer by any means. Hands-on management is required to "evangelize," recognize, reward, and review the use of information. Gates himself regularly reviews customer information provided by the sales forces, and regards this review by superiors as possibly "the biggest incentive... to keep our customer base up-to-date."

Investing in intellectual capital

The expenditure of his own time in the day-to-day business of Microsoft is justified by Gates as an investment in "intellectual capital," which he defines as "the intrinsic value of the intellectual property of your company and the knowledge your people have." In the "information society," the argument that intellectual capital is the only kind that counts has become a cliché. Behind the cliché, however, lies the reality that Gates sees reshaping the world – above all, the world of business.

Thomas A. Stewart, author of *Intellectual Capital* (1997), has written of "the end of management as we know it." Gates's efforts at Microsoft exemplify how the old-style approach to management must be changed in order to nurture the three varieties of intellectual capital, as described by Stewart, which are:

- Human (individual powers and resources)
- Structural (accumulated knowledge and know-how of the organization)
- Customer knowledge (which in Stewart's view is "probably... the worst managed of all intangible assets")

The human aspect of intellectual capital is not only concerned with the obvious knowledge worker, such as the programmer or Gates himself, but with turning others into knowledge workers. "In the new organization, the worker is no longer a cog in the machine but is an intelligent part of the overall process," writes Stewart. Computers, for example, are largely limited to the one-dimensional, repetitive work at which they excel. The excellence of human beings is needed to manage processes, rather than merely to execute tasks. And that creates knowledge workers, who use good digital information to play unique roles.

Developing, investing in, and deploying all this intellectual capital – knowledge management – surely goes beyond Gates's dismissal of the latter as "a fancy term for a simple idea." In fact, what he goes on to describe is far from simple in execution. "Your aim should be to enhance the way people work together, share ideas, sometimes wrangle, and build on one another's ideas – and then act in concert for a common purpose." That goal sounds like a managerial Utopia, something seen in only rare and fleeting circumstances, the heartfelt and generally frustrated desire of the CEO.

Raising the corporate IQ

As the CEO of Microsoft, Gates awards himself a specific role along the road to Utopia. His challenge is "raising the corporate IQ" in four ways:

- Establishing an atmosphere that promotes knowledge sharing and collaboration
- Prioritizing the areas in which knowledge sharing is most valuable
- Providing the digital tools that make knowledge sharing possible
- Rewarding people for contributing to a full flow of knowledge

The third of these keys to knowledge management is a greater challenge to managers who lack Gates's technological background than he recognizes. He writes about "sophisticated" applications of knowledge management (so much for simplicity). Many managers are still unfamiliar with tools such as databases, email, workflow applications, electronic files, and Web technology – the "building blocks" of knowledge management, in Gates's phrase. These digital tools must be applied in various combinations, although, as Gates explains, the technology is bringing together the separate richness of all digital tools "to make solutions much easier to build."

The easier the solutions, the nearer Utopian management will come to being realized. Gates points out that scientists have been using the Internet for far longer than managers, and that exchange of knowledge between scientists in different countries, together with "critiquing one another's thinking via email," have become matters of routine. He believes that, used in business, the same collaborative, knowledge-managing tools can significantly cut down research and development costs, improve the quality of new product thinking, speed the progress of the new offering to market, and dramatically reduce the incidence of failure.

Learning from your mistakes

Microsoft's own failures have not been forgotten but stored as part of the intellectual capital. This has only come about because the company is prepared to learn from the unfortunate past. Gates used to publish and revise annually a memo under the title "The Ten Great Mistakes of Microsoft." The object was not to wallow in error, but to stimulate "Microsofties" into learning the lessons. Many of the mistakes, according to Gates, came from entering markets either late or not at all.

Outsiders, however, might be more inclined to dwell on the software releases that were inadequate or faulty. In these cases, Microsoft certainly does learn from its own errors, simply because it has to correct them or lose the customers. But however much the "library" of knowledge about past programs builds up, however strongly the tools for software writing are standardized, however much brilliance is hired, the knowledge demands simply get more intimidating. In 1999 armies of Microsoft people were struggling to get the latest version of Windows to market, writing millions of lines of code and confronting an endless procession of bugs.

Maintaining market control

As Gates well understands, the process of acquiring knowledge and applying it to new purposes never ends. Not only do the mountains to climb get progressively higher but the landscape is constantly being changed by the hosts of other brains, at other companies and universities, who are taking different lines of knowledge to different conclusions. The Gates monopoly is commercial, not technological. That is why he places so much stress on obtaining and managing knowledge about the customer.

But there is a central difficulty for Microsoft as a learning organization. It cannot know everything about all customers, nor about all information technologies.

Much of its knowledge management is dedicated to maintaining the company's proprietary position. This position is vulnerable to technological developments that are not conceived or controlled by Microsoft. In some cases the new knowledge can be bought, by acquiring the business involved, or shared via a partnership agreement. Gates uses both approaches to deal with external intellectual challenges. But he is defending a minority position in the market for ideas. The knowledge company can never afford to relax.

Ideas into action

- Expect people to develop their personal capacity to excel.

- Build up the intellectual resources of the organization.

- Deploy and organize people to get maximum effectiveness of output.

- Use Websites to update knowledge and make it available.

- Hire smart people and keep them in touch with each other.

- Treat everybody as an intelligent part of the entire business.

- Obtain all the customer knowledge you can – and manage it.

Exploiting the info-revolution

Success in the future will depend very substantially on the Internet. That means understanding what Bill Gates calls the digital nervous system (DNS). At the same time, you must develop your ability to work in a "knowledge company" in which "knowledge management" is the key activity.

Understanding and using the DNS

The main benefits of the DNS are that it allows the same data to be used by teams simultaneously and provides up-to-the-minute information about customers and sales, thus enabling fast and appropriate response to customer needs and competitor challenges.

With the help of the DNS, Gates forced a massive shift in strategy at Microsoft, from sidelining the Internet to making it absolutely central to everything the company does and sells. Unquestionably, this is the kind of flexibility you will need in the years ahead.

Understanding the DNS and knowing how to apply its hardware and software to your management and business needs does not demand a high level of technical proficiency. If you can operate a typewriter keyboard and use a telephone, then you have the basic skills needed to exploit the DNS and manage knowledge.

Develop knowledge skills

There are four key skills that you will need, however, to become an efficient and effective knowledge manager. They are all concerned with the handling of information.

The Four Key Skills of the Knowledge Manager			
1 Understanding information	**2** Processing information	**3** Communicating information	**4** Correlating information

Think of yourself as a one-person company (Myself Inc.), and set out to become an effective practitioner of knowledge management. In other words, put into action on a personal scale the principles and practices of a knowledge company. Encourage everyone in the company to develop their full capacity. As individuals learn from each other – and the DNS – so the corporate intelligence increases.

BILL GATES

1 Learning the disciplines

As the first step in your personal development toward becoming a knowledge manager, identify the demands of the five "learning disciplines" outlined by Peter Senge (see p. 30).

The disciplines and your role

The example of Microsoft demonstrates how understanding and applying these disciplines leads to higher levels of performance. Relate the disciplines to your own role as a manager.

The Five Learning Disciplines
1 Developing your personal abilities
2 Applying the right "mind-set" to guide your performance
3 Committing yourself to the company's vision
4 Improving your team-thinking abilities
5 Understanding how your actions affect the whole organization

Raising your skills level

See yourself as a person with valuable skills – what Gates calls a "skills set" – and the ability to raise your skills level. Give yourself measurable, stretching, and valuable objectives to focus your mind on improving your performance and position.

Developing a Powerful Skills-set
Analyze your "skills set".
Match your skills to the requirements of your present job – and the job you want next.
Update your existing skills where necessary.
Enhance and augment those skills that you need to achieve your current and future objectives.
Start now!

Your personal vision

You need a vision both for yourself and for your business. This is the overarching idea that embraces all your specific objectives. Gates had a very powerful vision: "A PC on every desk and in every home, using Microsoft software." Your vision can be just as powerful.

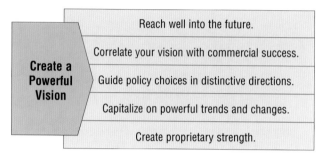

Create a Powerful Vision

Reach well into the future.

Correlate your vision with commercial success.

Guide policy choices in distinctive directions.

Capitalize on powerful trends and changes.

Create proprietary strength.

To reach your personal objectives – and realize your powerful vision – you also need the help of others.

Teamwork

Working in genuine teams (Senge's fourth discipline) is increasingly the norm. Team members need the same key skills, whether they are in a permanent or a temporary team. How good are your team skills? You should be able to answer "Yes" to these questions:

- Do you have one or more "partners" (people on whom you rely, and who rely on you, for complementary skills and advice)?
- Do you regard team leadership as "being the first among equals," rather than "being the boss"?
- Do you defer to colleagues, even of lower status, in the interests of achieving the team task?
- Do you align your personal objectives with those of the team?
- Do you ignore personalities and concentrate instead on people's actual contribution?

Looking at the whole picture

Systems thinking – Senge's fifth discipline – is another crucial managerial skill. It means thinking beyond the immediate: every action produces a reaction and every effect has side effects. Make sure you treat the root cause of any problem, not just the symptoms.

2 Using digital technology

The DNS is an excellent tool for two-way thinking. To make its
advantages work for you, seize every opportunity to learn how to use
the new technology to the full.

Exploit the DNS

Unlike other business technologies, the DNS is available to anyone –
and at an economic price. It has four key uses that together keep you
fully informed and up-to-date on a 24-hour basis.

Four Key Uses of the DNS
1 Producing, receiving, storing, accessing, and distributing documents and data of all kinds
2 Communicating and sharing information with other people anywhere in the world
3 Receiving "real-time", instant information about the operation and results of the business
4 Transacting business with customers and suppliers

While you can manage successfully without going near a screen, you
will work more reliably and cheaply if you make use of the new
technology. Find ways of replacing manual with digital means.

Conquer technophobia

If you are not an emailer, have not mastered spreadsheets, or cannot
use groupware to connect with others, ask yourself whether
technophobia is the cause. If so, eliminate it by:

■ Confronting the fear head-on
■ Finding out what hardware and software you need (both in the
office and on the move)
■ Obtaining all the equipment you require
■ Mastering the machines and programs through training
■ Using the technology intensively, until it becomes second nature
Do not leave the DNS to others, even the "experts." That will give
them a great advantage – and put you at a great disadvantage.

3 Managing your knowledge

Your success and failure, like those of a corporation, depend on how much intellectual capital you have and how well you use it. Keep looking for ways of working "smarter." The DNS can help you exploit and augment your intellectual capital.

Analyze your knowledge

In order to improve your intellectual capital, first you need to analyze your capabilities. Take an objective view by answering the following questions:

- What individual powers and resources do you possess? Taken together, how high do these score when measured on a scale of 1 (minimal) to 5 (excellent)?
- What knowledge have you accumulated about the organization, its businesses, and the market sector? How does this knowledge rate on a scale of 1 (shallow) to 5 (deep)?
- What special skills have you acquired during your career that you can use in your work? How do these skills rate on a scale of 1 (of minimal use in your work) to 5 (highly effective)?
- What do you know about your customers, both internal and external? How does this knowledge measure up on a scale of 1 (shallow) to 5 (deep)?
- On a scale of 1 (poorly) to 5 (very well), how effectively do you apply your individual powers and resources, your knowledge and special skills, and your overall understanding of the customer?

Analysis

If you have answered the questions honestly, there is likely to be a significant gap between the maximum rating score (25) and your final judgment of yourself. Use the results in a positive way to assess what your next step should be. Ask yourself how you can improve by:
- undertaking further training
- seeking wider experience
- becoming more effective inside and outside the organization.

Reassess yourself regularly

Acquiring and applying knowledge is a never-ending process, so run through the questions above every six months. The knowledge company can never afford to relax – and nor should you.

Knowledge sharing

Managing your own knowledge is only part of the picture. To create the collaborative culture that Gates encourages at Microsoft, you need to have a two-way exchange of ideas by:

- Pooling your knowledge with that of others – both in your own team and outside
- Taking steps to have the knowledge of others readily available
- Learning from an objective analysis of past and present successes and failures (especially the failures)
- Continually looking at the outside world, through all available media and contacts, to receive the stimulation of new knowledge and new ideas
- Developing ways to turn new knowledge and new ideas into new products, processes, services, and methods

Learn to succeed

As you analyze your own performance, do not be dismayed if you fall short of the ideals recommended by Gates. Remember that there is no such thing as perfection in the management and mobilization of knowledge – and Gates and Microsoft do make mistakes. But as Gates demonstrated in his annual memo listing the company's great mistakes, you can always learn to do better. By constantly seeking knowledge and turning it into profitable reality, you too can achieve phenomenal results.

Using the DNS to Turn Failure into Success

Microsoft's belated conversion to the Internet as a top priority is a classic demonstration of sharing knowledge and new ideas to turn failure into success.

The Internet comeback started with a memo from one man, J. Allard, in January 1994. A week later, Steven Sinovsky made a report on booming Internet use at Cornell University. The two memos "set off a fire-storm" of emails. The development plan and action items were made visible to everybody. Teams were set up to develop the email-driven thinking and analysis; then "retreats" fleshed out the priorities and coordinated the response. The first major progress review in August 1994 saw "the newer employees running the show" as problems were solved on the run. By early 1995 every team's task was defined. Says Gates: "our DNS informed and propelled" the strategy unveiled that December.

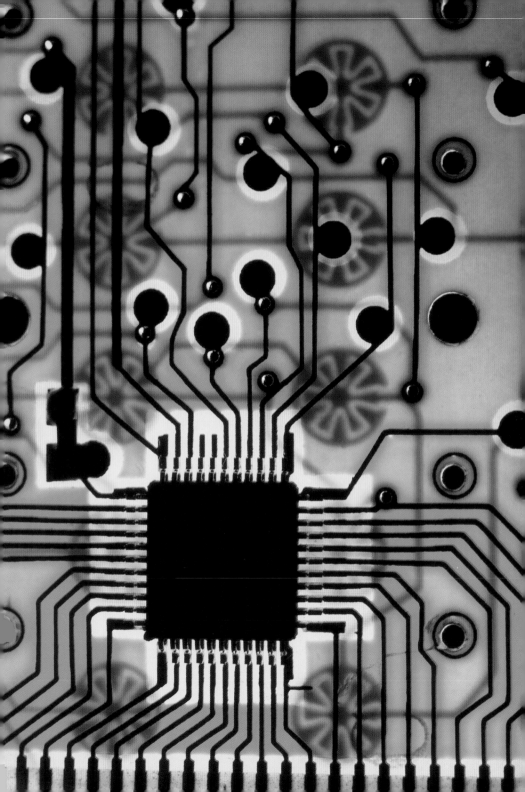

3

Developing software that sells

Organizing R & D around dedicated groups who concentrate on clear objectives ● **Making many technological bets to improve the chances of success** ● Why technology must be aimed at the highest possible targets ● **Making your product the best, most useful, and cheapest** ● Pursuing the continuous replacement of good products by something better ● **Managing technology to attain and sustain a dominant proprietary position** ● Translating great research into marketable products

Technology does not exist for its own sake, but for what it can do. At Microsoft, functionality is placed at the center of the research and development effort, which is organized around dedicated groups, who concentrate on clearly defined objectives. You do not seek breakthroughs, although you seize them with energy and enthusiasm if and when they arrive. You direct the effort at making major advances on your existing technological platforms – or other people's – to fulfill commercial aims. And you ensure that all necessary disciplines are available to you, preferably in-house.

This explains why, for example, Microsoft hired two husband-and-wife "statistical physicists" in 1997. *Fortune* magazine explained that they were seeking to "derive the observed behaviors of gases, liquids, solids, and other states of matter from the underlying microscopic worlds of molecules, atoms, and electrons." Their work involved the study of phenomena such as "independent percolation," which relates to "the distribution of oil in a porous medium to the distribution of matter in the galaxy."

Investing in research

Most research and development in the PC world is, in fact, development: basic research is rare, as it was at Microsoft until the late 1990s. Then Gates and his "chief technology officer," Nathan Myhrvold, began to build a chain of 645 researchers, placed at five centers around the world, including Microsoft headquarters in Redmond, Washington, and the famous university town of Cambridge in England.

Some of the brains assembled are very well known in microelectronics, including Gordon Bell, whose work on the VAX line of minicomputers for Digital Equipment

Creating the research lab
Gates meets Vice-Chancellor Professor Alec Broers and Professor Roger Needham of St. John's College, Cambridge, after investing $20 million in the computer research center at the university.

produced the world's first line of computers able to communicate easily with one another. Bell had, in fact, worked for Microsoft for some years before Gates decided to form "the next great research lab." He considered that $100 million a year was a relatively small investment in an enterprise that, one day, could pay off handsomely. Gates is mindful that the transistor sprang from research at Bell Laboratories, which was owned by the AT&T telecommunications giant.

Even more pertinent, today's PC, including the "graphical user interface," which made the Macintosh's operating system and Windows possible, was basically developed at the Palo Alto Research Center (PARC), founded and financed by Xerox Corporation. Obviously, such mighty breakthroughs are rare in the history of technology, let alone in that of any one company. But Gates believes in placing as many bets as possible, on the simple theory that this increases the chances of one bet winning colossally big. The bets, however, are carefully controlled – again on simple principles.

Directing research carefully

To determine an area of research you must first define a purpose on which to focus it. One of Microsoft's declared goals was to abolish the keyboard by enabling the PC to understand speech and to respond in speech. This led researchers into a number of disciplines: natural language processing, speech technology, user interface, and language-enabled applications. Because of its high value and wide scientific requirements, this project was assigned an especially large number of researchers in late 1997: 58, against a mere six trying to create better encryptions to make e-commerce more secure.

As it happens, Microsoft was beaten to the punch on the speech recognition project by other companies, including IBM, Dragon Systems, and Kurzweil, whose products were on sale while Microsoft was still researching. This is nothing new for Microsoft. Its research and development record has not been one of outstanding breakthroughs but of overhauling others by making more effective use of existing technology and then bringing more marketing muscle to bear. In 1992, Microsoft trailed Lotus in spreadsheets and WordPerfect in word processing. Microsoft's equivalent programs – Excel and Word – went on to surpass both by miles.

Joining research to commercial purpose is crucial, in Gates's view. He has fully learned the lesson of Xerox's astounding failure to market the PC developed at PARC. As Gates says, at PARC "the research was decoupled from product design": the PC technology could not find a commercial sponsor. At Microsoft Research, liaison with the product managers is a basic requirement. As an example, *Fortune* cites the independent researcher who, in 1995, developed a program that turned Internet chat into an interactive comic strip. A Microsoft product group heard of the idea, and took hold of both the research and the researcher to create Microsoft Chat 2.0.

A high degree of direction and organization (both of which come very naturally to Gates) is demanded by the sheer size of Microsoft's R & D operation. From the early days of Microsoft, Gates has practiced and preached the necessity of applying more than enough resources in manpower and money (which amount to the same thing) to solve the technological problems and supply the product needs. In late 1996, for example, he had 4,600 technologists working in the "platforms group," covering Windows, Explorer, and the other Internet applications. Another 1,800 were working on the desktop applications, which generated the highest profits.

Platforms cost Microsoft over $1 billion that year, desktop applications $400 million. Another $500 million went on

"... the tendency for successful companies to fail to innovate is just that: a tendency. If you're too focused on your current business, it's hard to look ahead...." *The Road Ahead*

projects, involving 2,000 technologists, that were not expected to contribute fully financially until the next millennium: these were interactive media, such as CD-ROM games and reference works, and online content. Then there was advanced technology and research, on which Microsoft spent a mere $25 million on 100 very expensive people, who were engaged in long-range research that might never pay off at all. Note the breakdown in the distribution of people: 75 percent on projects and products already generating vast profits, 24 percent on items expected to pay off in the near term, 1 percent on the bluer skies.

The disparity in money was equally striking: 20 times as much on interactive media as on speech synthesis and recognition and the other long-range research projects. The sheer quantity of the total effort is designed to be overwhelming. At the time when the Gates counterattack against Netscape had gathered full momentum, Microsoft's R & D staff numbered seven times more than the challenger's entire payroll, and the spending ran at nearly seven times Netscape's entire revenue.

Ambitious young partnership

Gates may not believe that success in managing technology is primarily a matter of massing men, women, and money, even though his actions certainly support that interpretation. His own experience would lead to a different conclusion: that quality counts for more than quantity. He and a friend from schooldays – Paul Allen – were in their early 20s and had just formed a partnership called Micro-Soft when Allen read about the first Intel microprocessor, the 4004. According to Gates, it was his partner who spotted the supreme importance of the invention — significantly, an unplanned by-product of Intel's unrelated work for a Japanese customer.

When Allen's belief, that the 4004 was only the beginning of major advances in microchip technology, proved true, the partners bought the greatly improved 8008 chip and used it for their first business project — Traf-O-Data — a program designed to help control Seattle's traffic. This project was unsuccessful. Moreover, it did not exploit the enormous potential of the microprocessor, which, Allen saw, promised far lower costs than conventional electronics. The partners concluded that their mistake had been to concentrate on "too narrow and challenging an area." They decided that in the future they would manage the new technology to hit the biggest possible targets. They then set their sights on nothing less than the whole market occupied by IBM and Digital Equipment.

Cofounder from school days
Like Bill Gates, Paul Allen was one of the group of computer geeks at Lakeside high school. In April 1975, he joined up with his old school friend to form a company called Micro-Soft.

Recognizing an opportunity

This might seem a breathtaking ambition. But even a small percentage of a vast market can mean huge income by start-up standards. Looking at the low cost and increasing power of microprocessors, "It seemed that [IBM and DEC] were screwed. We thought maybe they'd even be screwed tomorrow. We were saying, 'God, how come these guys aren't stunned? How come they're not just amazed and scared?'" Both those companies had access to the technology, better access than Gates and Allen by far, but the giants managed their technology toward a different destination: serving their existing corporate customers with their existing and constantly upgraded products.

Both companies had consequently missed the PC's precursors – the dedicated electronic word processors that made Wang rich. Wang in turn did not see (as Gates and Allen did) that general-purpose computers could process words and far more. But nobody at IBM or DEC, or Wang for that matter, had any great reason to take notice of the MITS Altair 8800: the "World's First Minicomputer Kit to Rival Commercial Models." That headline in *Popular Electronics* magazine in January 1975 inspired Gates and Allen to write a version of the well-known BASIC computer language for the machine to run on. They then persuaded MITS, a small Albuquerque company, to buy their version.

Later erroneous accounts describe Gates as having invented BASIC, which in fact he and Allen only adapted. This is the Gates pattern of technology management. Find an interesting technology and apply it to a new commercial purpose. Alternatively, find a new commercial purpose and look for the technology that will achieve it.

This second route became the dominant one for Microsoft. For example, the Japanese company Ricoh paid

Microsoft $180,000 to license every computer language the partners had – and then came back for more. Embarrassingly there wasn't any more. So Gates recalls asking, "What can we develop for you?" Ricoh responded with a list of software needs and Microsoft promised the company a package of products, including a word processor and a database. In reality the infant company could not deliver. They "had to go buy some of them from somebody else" – and even then the delivery was alarmingly late.

Competitive instinct

Sell now, make later became the established Microsoft pattern. It achieved its supreme moment with IBM, when two executives came to talk about buying Microsoft BASIC for the company's first PC (see p. 62). They took not only BASIC but two other languages. "It seemed just like Ricoh all over again," says Gates. "We had told IBM, 'Okay, you can have everything we make', even though we hadn't even made it yet." The two partners committed themselves to supplying IBM with an operating system two days before buying the necessary technology from another Seattle company.

At this point, another key element in Microsoft's successful business policy became critical: competitiveness. The Gates tenet is that being first is less important than being best, with best defined as providing the "biggest bang per buck" for the customer and for yourself.

DEVELOPING SOFTWARE THAT SELLS

"Getting in on the first stages of the PC revolution looked like the opportunity of a lifetime, and we seized it."
The Road Ahead

Setting the industry standard

F ew people know that two other operating systems were created for the IBM PC: one by Digital Research – then the leading producer of microcomputer software – and the UCSD Pascal P-System. Gates overcame this opposition with a three-point plan, which is an extraordinarily simple, decisively strong blueprint for success:

- Make your product the best.
- Make your product the most useful.
- Make your product the cheapest.

The greater utility was achieved by helping other software companies to write applications that would work on the MS-DOS platform. The cheapness came from charging IBM a mere $80,000 for a perpetual, royalty-free right to use MS-DOS. This meant that IBM could charge customers only $60 or so for MS-DOS, compared to $450 for the UCSD Pascal P-System and some $175 for the Digital product. It was no contest. As the number of PCs and MS-DOS applications rose, the Microsoft partners achieved their commercial objective. The IBM PC, using their operating system, became the industry standard.

If your technology becomes the standard, you are by definition the industry leader. When Gates sees another company's product in a leadership position, his immediate reaction is to seek to usurp that role. The approach has not always succeeded. Gates went after the network market, led by Novell, with Microsoft Network – and failed. When the same thing happened in personal finance software, where Microsoft Money came nowhere near Intuit, Gates sought (and failed) to buy the latter. His competitive urge remains a huge driving force. He seldom gives up. It took all of five years before Microsoft Exchange became a real competitor to Lotus Notes in groupware.

When survival is at stake, Gates shows at its most powerful the force of technology focus. The most recent and striking example was the launch of Explorer as an Internet browser in competition with the deeply entrenched and threatening Netscape. In less than a year from December 7 1995 to the autumn of 1996, Gates forced through the development of a product at least as good as Netscape's. He then gave the browser away. Just as with the IBM PC, Gates managed the price of the product to create market penetration, reasoning that if you possess the market, you eventually possess the profits.

Extending the power base

The operating system base gives Gates an inestimable advantage over his competitors. By bundling Microsoft applications with the operating software, Microsoft can in effect lock rivals out of the market. Gates cannot do this without the cooperation of the PC makers. But a circle develops (benevolent for Gates, vicious for the competition): the more popular Gates's software becomes, the greater the incentive for PC manufacturers to include the application programs in their package.

The temptation to reinforce this incentive by unfair commercial pressure is evident. The antitrust (monopoly) charges brought against Microsoft in 1998 were largely concerned with whether or not that temptation had been sufficiently resisted. As an exercise in managing technology, however, the use of the operating system as foundation has been a model. Gates has reinforced that model by his exploitation of technological improvement.

No other industry has possessed the technological engine that drives profit in microelectronics: that engine is the continuous replacement of a perfectly good product by something that is better. The American car manufacturers in the 1960s tried to achieve the same result of "planned obsolescence" with styling. But the PC hardware and software industries apply the same principle with the far more powerful means of higher functionality. From microprocessors via PCs to software, customers are driven to upgrade their purchases in a process that seems without end.

Safeguarding a position

This upgrading entered a new dimension when Gates decided, with the launch of Windows in 1985, to add a graphical interface to IBM-compatible PCs. Once again, the technology did not originate with Microsoft. As noted, the graphical user interface was developed at PARC by Xerox and first exploited by Apple in 1984, with the Macintosh. What became two enormously lucrative Microsoft applications – Word and Excel – were also originally developed for the Mac. Microsoft's work with Apple on applications helped Gates to find a wonderful escape route from a joint product with IBM – OS/2, the operating system that was intended to replace MS-DOS.

While Microsoft has been and is involved in innumerable partnerships, its technology has always been managed to sustain its proprietary position – what it sells, it owns. That sovereign principle would not have applied with OS/2, a new system intended to protect and enhance the proprietary strength of IBM. Gates claims that all along the strategy of outflanking IBM never entered his mind. But the Windows strategy, in hindsight, has been even more beneficial to

Gates than his original IBM alliance. Again, tenacity was required: "The success of Windows was a long time coming," Gates acknowledges.

The delay was as much with applications providers as with customers. But as Windows won acceptance, the Microsoft applications, such as Word and Excel, after being developed to work with Windows, overtook products that did not. Reflecting upon this and other experiences, Gates has observed, accurately enough, that "translating great research into products that sell is still a big problem for many companies." In his case, it is the translation, rather than the greatness of the research, that has been decisive.

Ideas into action

- Assemble the best brains you can find for product development.

- Concentrate people and money on the most promising R & D objectives.

- Try to find interesting technologies and apply them to new purposes.

- Try to find new purposes and look for appropriate technology to fulfill them.

- Aim to give the customer the "biggest bang per buck."

- Seek ways to make your product indispensable to the buyers.

- Persevere tenaciously with new products until you get them right.

Making MS-DOS central to the IBM PC

Among all the sagas of start-up triumph, that of Bill Gates and Microsoft trumps them all. The pivotal moment came in 1980 when two IBM emissaries arrived in Seattle to quiz the infant firm about its software.

They initially talked about buying the Microsoft version of the BASIC language for the still-secret PC project. But when the IBMers went on to discuss two other languages, Gates told them, "okay, you can have everything we make." The major issue for the partners was whether to offer IBM an operating system as well. Although Gates was a little reticent, "we decided, why not?"

They had been talking to a local firm, Seattle Computer Products, about its Q-DOS (Quick and Dirty Operating System), which they thought could "probably" be adapted for IBM's purposes. To hold Seattle Computer Products' price for Q-DOS down to as little as $50,000, they kept IBM's interest secret from the vendor (they also poached its chief engineer, Tim Patterson). The partners then offered IBM a perpetual license to use the operating system, with no royalties, for only $80,000.

With both deals done, the partners started working day and night, not just on the software, which they renamed MS-DOS (Microsoft Disk Operating System), but also on the design of the PC. According to Gates, although working with IBM engineers, "by the end Paul [Allen] and I decided every stupid little thing about the PC: the keyboard layout, how the cassette port worked, how the sound port worked, how the graphics port worked."

They also successfully (and critically – leapfrogging the competition from Apple) encouraged IBM to use a more powerful, 16-bit chip. Although the pair got $186,000 for their contribution, they were not even invited to the official launch of what (to IBM's surprise, but not that of Gates) was the biggest instant hit in computing history.

Central force

Gates had a far stronger perspective on that history than IBM. To the latter, the PC was an "entry-level" product that would justify itself by leading on to sales of larger computers. To Gates, it

> **"... we practically gave the software to IBM. Giving software away to create strategic value has since become a well-established marketing technique in the industry, but it was uncommon at the time."**
> *The Road Ahead*

was the birth of a whole new world. "We could see that, with its reputation and its decision to employ an open design that other companies could copy, IBM had a real chance to create a new, broad standard in personal computing." Without that standard, the coming of Gates's vision – a computer on every desk and in every home – would be long delayed. With that standard, all his ambitions for Microsoft and the PC revolution could be realized.

It took only a year for Microsoft to oust the two other operating systems initially offered on the IBM PC (see p. 58). Gates today refutes the widely held view that Microsoft "somehow got the better of IBM," and that the latter should have taken full ownership of MS-DOS. Gates argues that the deal, which left Microsoft free to supply all IBM's rivals, enabled IBM to become "the central force in the PC industry." He is being disingenuous. That central force proved to be Microsoft.

Mastering the business

Bill Gates's career teaches unbeatable lessons in business management. Although he built his fortune on highly technical products, his business mastery is even more important than his technical skills. By using his basic strategy, you can emulate Microsoft's success in your company – and yourself.

Compete for success
Whatever business you are in, the principles for achieving market dominance are the same. Master your own market, using the six-part competitive strategy:

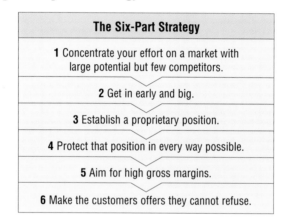

The Six-Part Strategy

1 Concentrate your effort on a market with large potential but few competitors.

2 Get in early and big.

3 Establish a proprietary position.

4 Protect that position in every way possible.

5 Aim for high gross margins.

6 Make the customers offers they cannot refuse.

The early success of Gates and his partner, Paul Allen – the result of supreme ambition grounded in reality – was founded on this strategy. It can be applied to anything from high-tech products to sausages – as long as they are a new, inimitable kind of sausage. Use technological advances to achieve non-technical commercial aims.

Plan strategically
The best strategies aim to give you a position of clear "competitive advantage" such as that that Gates enjoys. Use the matrix on the right to analyze your own strategy. Which of your products fits into which square? "Different and better" is by far the best.

Different and better	Different and worse
The Same and worse	The Same and better

BILL GATES

Go for the best

For Gates, being the best is more important than being the first. Customers want "the biggest bang per buck" and will usually pay more for something that they perceive as better. Gates believes that you should continually invest resources in research and development to get the right products, and develop your products and services to find ways in which they can be constantly improved.

While not all Microsoft's products have achieved market leadership, in general they have been seen as sufficiently different – and effective – to support the quasi-monopoly that the company obtained through its connection with IBM.

Following the principles

Note the way in which Gates and Allen won that contract. These two absurdly young and confident entrepreneurs perfectly applied the six-part strategy outlined opposite:

- They pursued a potentially huge market (built on IBM's PC sales), in which they faced only two competitors.
- They got in first, even though they originally had no product.
- They kept the proprietary right to sell to anybody and everybody.
- They protected their IBM position by charging the lowest price for their product.
- They earned a high gross margin on sales to third parties.
- They made IBM an offer it could not refuse – a perpetual license to use MS-DOS, with no royalties.

Outwitting IBM

Gates and Allen gained a tremendous advantage from riding on the coattails of IBM, which made it much easier to pursue the six-point strategy.

Early on, Gates and Allen realized that the microcomputer would become powerful enough to challenge IBM. They dedicated themselves to ensuring success for IBM's PCs, knowing full well that "there were going to be clones." They "structured that original contract to allow them. It was a key point in the negotiations."

When IBM sought to attack the clones with new PCs and software, since Gates had to carry on working with IBM, he "sunk hundreds of millions of dollars" and countless worker-hours into the OS/2 joint venture. That folded in 1992, but Gates had won time to develop Windows. As a bonus, one OS/2 product became Windows NT.

1 Applying the strategy

At the outset, Microsoft's position was exceptionally favorable. The company entered on the ground floor of an industry of inexhaustible growth, and worked with a giant that depended entirely on outsiders such as Gates and Allen to make its PC project succeed.

Launching a business

You may not be able to make your fortune as easily as Gates and Allen did, but you can save yourself from losing one by asking yourself the same questions that Microsoft answered. Will you:

- Have a large enough market – now and in the probable future?
- Win a big enough share of the market to make a major impact on your business?
- Get in early enough?
- Be able to sustain a big enough effort?
- Establish a proprietary position that is based on being different and better?
- Be able to protect that position from challenge?
- Earn high gross margins at economical prices?
- Offer the customers a unique deal?

Many businesses launch ventures without posing these questions, let alone answering them. You need to be able to answer "Yes" to all eight questions. This may not be possible immediately – at first, Gates and Allen did not know whether their purchased product would work well enough for IBM's purposes. But going through the questions and changing your plans where necessary is an invaluable exercise. Approach it in a realistic but optimistic spirit: you are not trying to kill your idea but working to make it succeed.

Staying ahead

Keep asking the questions again and again as markets change and new technologies and new competitors arrive. Gates offers textbook examples of how to reposition your strategy as circumstances change; for example, breaking the umbilical cord with IBM, or reversing his stand on the Internet. Never allow past successes to lull you into a sense of security. The lesson is a hard one to master, but simple to remember: "If at first you *do* succeed, try, try again."

2 Building the brand

Every business is a "brand": the sum total of the perceptions of all its customers, employees, suppliers, etc. Work on achieving brand excellence for your company, and also for your personal "brand."

Focus on performance

To achieve brand excellence, performance is far more important than publicity. Gates won with the Windows brand by spotting an idea (from Apple) and acting on it. You can follow in his footsteps.

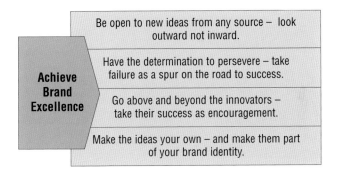

Achieve Brand Excellence

- Be open to new ideas from any source – look outward not inward.
- Have the determination to persevere – take failure as a spur on the road to success.
- Go above and beyond the innovators – take their success as encouragement.
- Make the ideas your own – and make them part of your brand identity.

As a manager, you clearly need to achieve, support, and strengthen brand excellence in every way you can. But remember this applies not only to your business, but to your own "brand": the perceptions that others have of you and your performance. Think of yourself as "Myself Inc.," and apply to yourself the same brand-building strategy. Apply the four strategic aspects to your own personal career: they are highly effective.

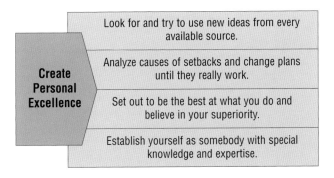

Create Personal Excellence

- Look for and try to use new ideas from every available source.
- Analyze causes of setbacks and change plans until they really work.
- Set out to be the best at what you do and believe in your superiority.
- Establish yourself as somebody with special knowledge and expertise.

3 Leading decisively

Business success depends ultimately on leadership. But as a manager you have to grasp two apparently contradictory principles. Give clear command from the top, but harness as much collective effort as you can from all ranks of the organization.

Involving people

It is particularly important to get everyone involved if yours is a high-tech business, because you cannot possibly master all the technical knowledge – or do all the work – on your own. The key is to practice both "soft" and "hard" management.

The "soft" management approach

The soft style of management, which has influenced the open culture in Microsoft, focuses on collective effort. You should:

- Encourage a free-and-easy atmosphere.
- Create a flat structure with few levels of hierarchy.
- Split the company into small groups.
- Give groups well-defined tasks for which they are completely responsible.
- Encourage discussion and debate (especially by using email).
- Recognize and reward individual and team successes.

If your company does not have such an atmosphere, resist its rigidities as best you can.

The "hard" management approach

A proper exercise of control from the top is fundamental to effective management. Everyone in the company needs to know who exercises authority in each area of the organization.

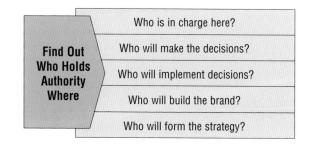

Find Out Who Holds Authority Where	
	Who is in charge here?
	Who will make the decisions?
	Who will implement decisions?
	Who will build the brand?
	Who will form the strategy?

Delegating leadership

In Microsoft's case, the clear answer to every question, before the 1999 restructuring, was Bill Gates. Somebody, to use a Gates phrase, must be capable of an "act of leadership." But many other people can and must contribute before any final decision is made. The issue is how widely and deeply the leader delegates, and how big a part he or she plays before having the last word.

Giving autonomy

In the Microsoft restructuring, eight autonomous divisions were established under separate managers. Giving them the authority to lead was partly designed to stop Gates continuing to take on too much himself, which had the effect of slowing down the decision-making process at Microsoft to an alarming degree.

To stop that happening to you, make sure that you apply the five Es that are basic to Microsoft. It will create an atmosphere in which everybody can contribute to success, and which motivates and stretches everybody, including you.

Applying The Five Es
1 EMPOWER people to undertake tasks for which they are competent and to see those tasks through from start to finish.
2 Adopt an EGALITARIAN attitude toward everybody, and insist that they do likewise.
3 Place an extraordinary EMPHASIS on performance, first making clear precisely what is expected.
4 Use ELECTRONIC means to send and receive messages to and from anybody, and maintain continuous, open, constructive debate on issues of interest or importance.
5 ENRICH people with rewards for success, using not only financial rewards but also praise and recognition.

If you are not already working in a five-E company, reconsider your position. Decide whether you – and your staff – are able to give of your best, and whether your effort is recognized. If not, think seriously about moving Myself Inc. to a new home.

4

Dividing, delegating, and leading

Why even the most successful companies must reinvent themselves ● **How managing with the force of facts requires information technology** ● Five people e-policies: enrichment, egalitarianism, emphasis on performance, email, empowerment ● **Using email to get simultaneous debate of issues at many levels** ● Achieving a small-company culture by dividing to keep units small ● **Why Microsoft is always two years away from crisis** ● Exploiting opportunities and leading decisively

In the spring of 1999, Bill Gates's approach to management underwent a crucial change. The company was split into eight new divisons, each run by executives who, in theory, had all the autonomy required to manage their empires. The reorganization was required to implement "Vision Version 2" ("VV2"), which reorients Microsoft from personal computers to all forms of information software and hardware, and focuses the company around the needs of customers. As Gates explained, "Even the most successful companies must constantly reinvent themselves."

Until VV2, though, the Microsoft management style had not been invented, in the sense of deliberate planning. It inevitably reflected the personality of its founders, Gates in particular. He first established a working relationship with Paul Allen, and then went on to surround himself with people and systems who suited his personal style.

Learning to manage

In the early days of Microsoft, the style was "a little loose," in Allen's words. The partners shared every decision and alternated tasks so often that who did what remained unclear. Allen, however, tended toward the new technology and new products, and Gates toward "negotiations and contracts and business deals." The division of labor is interesting in view of Gates's later reputation as the supreme nerd, the man to whom technology is all.

At Microsoft, the technology is managed toward well-defined business ends, acquiring and retaining customers, and creating and defending profit streams. The systems, largely digital, on which the organization runs, have evolved according to need and are not based on any theory.

That's understandable when you consider that, as managers, the pair were largely self-taught, with experience their main teacher. Gates recalls their approach: "Okay, we have to hire people; so what do we do? Okay, we're going to rent space; how do we do that? Okay, we're going to do contracts with people now; I'd get advice from my dad." William Henry Gates II was a leading corporate lawyer in Seattle, so the advice was undoubtedly sound.

Founding management style

Gates and Allen were very bright, "super-smart" computer geeks, people who could take a computer apart, write software, and understand new technology. As they developed management skills on top of their technical expertise, they sought other technical experts, some of whom, over time, would likewise evolve into managers. Hiring managers is not Microsoft's way. Even today the company hires people for their ability as marketers, programmers, content providers. Microsoft management is highly professional, but it is inseparable from other professional skills – much as in the early days.

Two other lasting features of Microsoft management style also developed during the early days. Decisions were made in very long discussions – known as "marathons" – that lasted for six to eight hours. They are still a regular occurrence today. And the pair expected others to copy their habit of working extremely hard and long. Gates has never lost the habit. One awesome description of his progress on a world tour in 1997 reveals an extraordinary ability to cram a host of activities into the day, with no time wasted, and with the main objective – selling more Microsoft software – never escaping from sight.

Sloan as role model

Hard work and long hours, however, do not explain how to manage a company doubling every 18 months and employing (at the end of 1998) 30,000 people. Gates is evidently a highly competent manager who employs competent subordinates and deploys them effectively. But "management" does not figure in the index of either of his books. Nor is Gates featured as a role model in management studies. That is probably because Gates does not subscribe to any particular management theories or follow any role model himself – with the exception of the long-dead Alfred P. Sloan, the man who made General Motors great.

What impressed Gates about Sloan (as gleaned from the latter's *My Years at General Motors*, 1963) was his "positive, rational, information-focused leadership." Gates is especially interested in the personal attention that Sloan paid to the dealer network, and his use of a standardized accounting system that gave every dealer and every employee "categorized numbers in precisely the same way." Sloan's personal visits to dealers (imitated by Gates in his world tours) appealed to Gates's constant urge to sell software. As for the reporting, that feeds his business, too. "To manage with the force of facts...," writes Gates, "requires information technology."

Until 1999, Gates had never publicly shown any interest in the structural principles that Sloan famously applied to

"It's inspiring to see in Sloan's account of his career how positive, rational, information-focused leadership can lead to extraordinary success."
Business @ the Speed of Thought

turn a sprawling bunch of car companies into an organized and highly effective corporation. The VV2 reorganization, however, follows Sloan's principles to the letter, dividing the company into separate business groups and, says Gates, "holding the leaders of our new business divisions accountable to think and act as if they are independent businesses." The crucial issue here is whether Gates and his recently named president, Steve Ballmer, can stand aside enough to allow their managers genuine independence of thought and action.

According to *Business Week* (August 1999), before VV2, with "decisions large and small being funneled to the top, the pair became a bottleneck." This contributed to Microsoft's "snail's pace for decision making." Compared to the hectic pace of the Internet world, Microsoft had begun to look "sluggish, even bureaucratic." The reorganization aimed "to free Microsoft from its bureaucratic morass" and to free executives from a constant top-down scrutiny that "undermined the confidence of managers below."

Management involvement

The reality of the pre-VV2 Microsoft is expressed by a former top officer at Microsoft, Mike Maples: if Gates or other senior managers "want to review where the teams are, [they] can ask to do so." They not only could, they did. Maples noted that the teams "never have to wait until they've been reviewed... they just go from start to finish by themselves." But that only happened if the senior managers did not get involved: mostly they did, and some considerable top involvement will surely remain basic to Microsoft management. On his own estimate, before VV2 Gates was spending 70 percent of his time on reviewing teams, holding two or three such meetings a day, keeping numbers low, and running the discussions in an informal, non-hierarchical, but highly penetrating, business-oriented style.

Gates inadvertently reveals how much he and other top people have been accustomed to intervene – or interfere – in passages from *Business @ the Speed of Thought* that are designed to show Microsoft management at its best. In these accounts, Gates tells how he met with headquarters colleagues to look closely at the "numbers" of all the overseas subsidiaries; how he got involved in a change to the way these "financials" were reported to give him a faster, clearer picture; and how he conducted executive reviews to consider, for example, the detail of a project to identify the best US cities for a new marketing campaign.

Until a customer CEO advised him to stop, Gates even passed top people's expense accounts, including Ballmer's. He knew all about the system for hiring, managing, and paying temporary staff – and so on. All this immersion in operating detail, however, is now supposed to belong to the past. The leaders of the eight divisions are enfranchised to exercise autonomous authority over operations, reporting to Ballmer.

Microsoft people policies

This new empowerment adds a fifth E to the four that are well-established aspects of Microsoft's basic people policies. The five Es are:

- Enrichment
- Egalitarianism
- Emphasis on performance
- Email
- Empowerment

Enrichment recruits, motivates, and retains people, not through high salaries but by the prospect of large capital gains. When employees are rewarded with the stock of the century, this wealth must be a potent means of binding them to the company and binding the company together. Egalitarianism treats all employees as equal and largely ignores all behaviors except for performance, which is (in both senses) highly stressed. In his book, *Company Man* (1995), Anthony Sampson quotes an employee's description of the egalitarian approach: "They're not interested in your clothes, your style, or when and how you work: you can work at home all the time. But they're sure interested in what you produce. They review your progress twice a year, with marks from one to five. Four means exceptional; one means you're out."

What Sampson calls "a casual, egalitarian style" fits Gates like a glove. The glove, as the above quote indicates, conceals an iron fist; that is, the emphasis on performance. You do not work for Microsoft unless you are prepared to work a 60-hour week at times, and in exceptional times, 100 hours or more. Nor do you live high: when the chairman and CEO travels economy class (business class only on international flights), you do not fly higher than the billionaire – even if you are a millionaire yourself. The millions used not to affect employee retention, either: the possessors could all retire, and now some choose to.

Using email purposefully

The former high loyalty survived Gates's abrasive style and very open intolerance of what he calls "stupid" thinking. His fierce criticism is expressed both verbally and through the fourth distinguishing factor of Microsoft management: electronic mail. The use of email, according to Mike Maples, helps to accomplish several of Gates's management polices, which are:

- Eliminate politics, by giving everybody the same message.
- Keep a flat organization in which all issues are discussed openly.
- Insist on clear and direct communication.
- Prevent competing missions or objectives.
- Eliminate rivalry between different parts of the organization.
- "Empower" teams to do their own thing.

Maples adds that email "encourages people at multiple levels to enter the debate simultaneously, so you don't have to have a workgroup debate an issue, take it to the manager, debate the issue again, take it to another manager, for more debate, and filter it up the chain of command. Instead, decision making happens in real time with people at all levels in the organization." That organization is dedicated, according to its founder, to the quest for an "atmosphere in which creative thinking thrives and employees develop to the fullest potential."

Small-company dynamic

Gates achieves this culture, he writes, by the "way Microsoft is set up... you have all the incredible resources of a large company yet you still have that dynamic small-group, small-company feeling where you can really make a difference." He envisages this set-up as a form of dialogue. The individuals produce ideas, and Microsoft responds by making it possible for those ideas to become reality. "Our strategy has always been to hire strong, creative employees, and delegate responsibility and resources to them so they can get the job done," adds Maples.

To achieve the small-company culture, Gates keeps units small. As soon as a team gets beyond a comfortable size (say, 30 people), it is divided. Gates is a believer in controllable size and in "project management," in which you place tasks under leaders who in turn subdivide the task among subordinates who work in a coordinated program to achieve the desired result. Gates then encourages constructive controversy between the divided parts of the corporation, and cements the latter with a central vision as well as personal enrichment – rewarding success but swiftly penalizing failure.

Managing change

The constant formation of new units is one means of gearing up for change. Gates sees Microsoft as an agent of transformation in a society that has reached an "inflection point." He says that "the human experience is about to change." "The transition will be exciting and historic, empowering to individuals and brutal to some companies and institutions that don't keep pace." According to Gates, if you do not practice the change management that looks after the future, the future will not look after you. And you dare not miss the moment: "Once certain thresholds are crossed, the way we work and live will change – forever," he warns.

Gates has said that Microsoft is always two years away from crisis; that is, failure to react to discontinuous change. The experience of nearly missing the explosive take-off of the Internet (see p. 106) has not been forgotten: "That kind of crisis is going to come up every three or four years," he acknowledges. His recipe for dealing with discontinuous change is to "try and make sure today's not the day we miss the turn in the road. Let's find out what's going on in speech recognition or in artificial intelligence. Let's make sure we're hiring the kinds of people who can pull those things together, and let's make sure we don't get surprised."

The new preface of the second edition of his first book, *The Road Ahead* (1996), gives Gates's views on change: "I work in the software industry, where change is the norm. A popular software title, whether it's an electronic encyclopedia, a word processor, or an online banking system, gets upgraded every year or two with major new features and continuous refinements. We listen to customer feedback and study new technology opportunities to determine the improvements to make." But this, of course, is not discontinuity: it is the continuous improvement that the Japanese call *kaizen*.

What forced Gates's about turn on the Internet was what the Japanese call *kaikaku*, or radical change, or "sea changes," as they are known at Microsoft. Gates told Geoffrey James, author of *Giant Killers* (1997), that the "most important and exciting part of my work as chairman is recognizing [sea changes] and articulating the opportunities they present to each person in the company.

"One thing is clear: we don't have the option of turning away from the future.... No one can stop productive change in the long run because the marketplace inexorably embraces it." *The Road Ahead*

We then empower employees with as much information and as many productivity tools as possible, so they can achieve results within the framework of that vision."

Decisive leadership

That key element of Gates's role as CEO – taking all the big strategic decisions – will surely continue. *The Wall Street Journal* pieced together a full account of how Gates handled the discussion on a crucial issue: should Microsoft continue with Windows, using that as an entry point for the Internet, or should it launch a "cross-platform" replacement, using Java software, that would run on all computers – as many corporate customers wanted? For months the opposing camps wrangled over email, exemplifying Gates's principle of letting people fight issues out.

Then, in March 1997, a meeting of top managers heard Gates deliver his verdict. He did not "discuss" the Java idea: he shot it down in flames. "In no uncertain terms, Mr. Gates had decided to protect Windows at all costs," the article concluded. The 2,000 employees in the Internet group were "reassigned," and two key teams were returned to the Windows group. This vital decision was implemented with a massive drive to take the Web browser market from Netscape by bundling Microsoft's rival Explorer with Windows – a strategy that backfired in the antitrust action of 1998 (see p. 59).

Important Microsofties were badly bruised by the decision: the losing senior executive in this struggle had previously masterminded the enormously profitable launch of Windows 3.0. The strategy could also still backfire in the marketplace, if rival attempts to launch a cross-platform attack on Windows should succeed. But the episode demonstrates five central principles in Gates's theory and practice of management. They are:

- The boss is the boss.
- As boss, he listens to all opposing arguments, and then makes a clear, unarguable decision.
- He makes sure that the decision is followed through.
- The boss concentrates on solutions that will best protect and profit the company's proprietary position.
- He takes the decision that embodies the best trade-off between risk and return.

Keeping the wheel turning

Gates's role is not so much "recognizing sea changes and articulating the opportunities they present" as exerting leadership. Spotting major trends is part of leadership, but only part. Gates will speak of an "act of leadership," meaning that he takes charge and wills what he wants to happen. But "leadership," like "management," does not figure in Gates's writings. That is because he is not interested in the theory of leadership, only in its practice. Without this particular leader, however, the Microsoft wheel would lack its vital hub. Would it keep turning?

The system easily surmounted the early retirement of Paul Allen. Gates says: "my best business decisions have had to do with picking people. Deciding to go into business with Paul Allen is probably at the top of the list, and subsequently, hiring a friend – Steve Ballmer – who has been my primary business partner ever since." This partnership with somebody totally trusted and totally committed, with the same vision, but some difference in skills, is the only balance to the total decision power of the chief executive.

Gates sums up the partner's role: "Some of the ideas you run past him, you know he's going to say, 'Hey, wait a minute, have you thought about this and that?'" While the point is true and valuable, Gates's words do not suggest that he gets tremendous opposition, even from this source. He argues that he and his top managers spend time talking about succession issues, and the importance of growth in making Microsoft "able to spawn off very, very big jobs for people." But the question must be whether the biggest job of all isn't too big – even after the implementation of Vision Version 2 – for anybody except Bill Gates.

Ideas into action

- Hire the brightest people with the greatest specific "skills sets."

- Improve management information to get exactly what you need – fast.

- Treat everybody as a close colleague from whom you expect plenty.

- Keep the organization flat, using email to debate issues openly.

- Watch out for radical change, and change radically to meet it.

- Keep teams small and delegate responsibility and resources to make them effective.

- When it's time to lead, make sure you lead decisively.

Making a success
of Windows NT

The story of Windows NT shows the Gates philosophy working at its best. This operating system, designed to take sophisticated (corporate) users into the 21st century, came out in 1993 and was an instant flop.

Windows NT missed its targets and market so badly that wags called it "Windows Not There." Any conventional management would have given up then and there, and withdrawn the product. But one of Gates's major principles is that you never give up without a fight, and, if you fight well enough, you won't need to give up at all.

Three years on, Microsoft had established Windows NT as one of its key products and major growth areas: a billion-dollar business whose sales doubled in 1996 and have soared ever since. The winning approach exemplifies another pillar of Gates's philosophy. Give the problem to the best person you can find and tell the appointee to fix it in their own way. A key Microsoft executive, Jim Allchin, NT's chosen savior, has observed: "some other companies would have said, 'I give up'." Instead, the NT team used failure as the springboard for recovery.

This attitude accords perfectly with the view of a previous king of computing, Thomas Watson of IBM, who remarked: "That's where success is. On the far side of failure." Allchin systematically established connections with the engineers and customers who had been woefully neglected during the $500 million development program for NT. He reacted to every criticism, including those in the trade press, not with denial, but with immediate action. As the software improved, corporate buyers were won over – and NT's subsequent triumph has been founded on the booming market for servers.

Taking decisive action

The difficulty of getting acceptable technical performance was very considerable: for example, 16 programmers had to be hired just to quicken little pieces of the NT code. Gates has a false reputation as a technological genius. He is not. It was the non-technical triple whammy of

knowing what to do, knowing how to do it, and actually doing it that produced the NT bonanza. Without that, Gates would have been far worse positioned for his Internet strategy (see p. 106). NT has 38.3 percent of the market in operating systems for corporate networks and Web servers. The penetration is far below Microsoft's 90 percent of the PC operating systems and applications market. But without NT and its overdue successor, the Windows 2000 application, Gates could not hope to master the market for large Websites and corporate computing centers. And Windows 2000 has been another model of persistence – five years in the making.

"Once you embrace unpleasant news not as a negative but as evidence of a need for change, you aren't defeated by it. You're learning from it." *Business @ the Speed of Thought*

Similar benefit is available to any manager in any industry who is prepared to recognize harsh reality, take criticism on the chin, and act on the corollary to Murphy's Law. The law states that "whatever can go wrong, will." The Gates corollary says that "whatever goes wrong can be made right." Don't deny, bite the bullet, and even abject failure can be turned into success.

Making the future happen

A *"vision" is a call to action. The original Bill Gates vision – "a PC on every desk and in every home, using Microsoft software" – was specific, highly ambitious, and clearly linked to the company. It contrasts strongly with the vague visions drawn up by many large companies. Follow Microsoft's example and invent your own future.*

Get ahead of the game

The purpose of a vision is to train your sights on achieving a future that is better than your present – not by small degrees but by orders of magnitude. With this mind-set you (like Gates) win an enormous advantage over other people who are not purposeful and progressive. Draw up your own vision:

- Take a piece of paper.
- Write across the top where you want yourself (and/or your business) to be in no less than five years' time.
- Write across the bottom – with merciless accuracy – where you are right now.
- Fill the space in-between with the steps you need to take in order to move from the bottom of the page to the top.

The whole exercise should take no more than an hour, though you may well find that the most difficult part of the task is starting.

Make things happen

A lot of managers are reluctant to take part in this exercise. If this includes you, ask yourself why:

- Are you just unambitious?
- Do you find it hard to think ahead?
- Are you reluctant to confront hard truths about the present?
- Are you put off by the major tasks and hard work that may be needed to create your future?
- Do you just prefer simply to wait on events?

If Gates and Allen had answered "yes" to any of these questions, the Microsoft phenomenon would never have been born. Be ambitious about your goals, think about the future, learn to face realities, and be prepared to work hard to make things happen.

1 Setting your goals

Do you set evolutionary or revolutionary goals? In fact, to be successful, you must do both. Improve your products or services on a continuous basis to remain competitive, and launch totally new products or services to seize the chance of winning big.

Go for mega-aims

Most R&D at Microsoft has involved evolutionary improvement. You also need to look for better ways of doing what you are doing already. But mega-prizes are only possible with mega-aims: what have been called "big, hairy audacious goals."

Recognizing Big, Hairy Audacious Goals
They make a very large difference to future success.
They stretch you well beyond the present levels of achievement.
They involve a considerable degree of risk.
They include major tasks that you have never previously accomplished.
They appear "impossible" in the eyes of others, including competitors.

Revolutionize your thinking

Typical examples of audacious goals at Microsoft were the offer of MS-DOS for the IBM PC, and the investment in Windows and Internet Explorer. Each of these developments set the organization in a new direction and radically changed its prospects.

Big, hairy, audacious goals may look frightening at first sight. But sometimes investing in them is the only way you can reach your revolutionary destination. Act without fear:

- Exploit the exceptional motivation of the big prize.
- Grab opportunities that you might otherwise have missed.
- Approach new tasks with new ideas.

Remember that you can often achieve far more than you actually expect of yourself. In addition, the perceived "impossibility" of your audacious goals will deter many other companies from competing effectively against you.

2 Managing by fear

To make the future happen, you need confidence: but fear is also valuable. It is a vital element in Gates's approach to business. He regards Microsoft as an underdog. Emulate his attitude: fear the competition, and you will be unlikely to fall into complacency.

Believe in the opposition

Many managers are all too eager to write off the competition. That leads them either to delay response or, still worse, not to respond at all. It is very dangerous to underestimate competitors. On the contrary, you should always believe that the opposition is capable of:

- Doing the impossible
- Defeating you
- Destroying your success

When Microsoft attacked the browser market, which was totally occupied by Netscape, the latter believed that the attack could never succeed. But with Netscape charging for Navigator, Microsoft offered Explorer for free. Had Netscape responded to the challenge by immediately abandoning its prices, Microsoft Explorer would have faced a far harder task.

Stay ahead of the game

Even more damaging, Netscape did not maintain a clear product lead over Explorer: it failed to make evolutionary improvements. Failure to keep updating and improving your product runs unacceptable risks. It may make recovery difficult, if not impossible. To avoid this situation in your own business, keep asking your customers (not yourself) how well or badly they rate the products or services you offer – in detail.

Ask Your Customers for Their Views

What attributes of my product and/or service do you value?
How do you rank these attributes in order of importance?
How do you rate my product and/or service against the competition (on all attributes)?

Keeping ahead

This analysis will immediately show where you have an advantage over the competition. But you can only keep one step ahead of the competition by deciding how to add value for your customers.

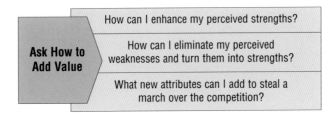

Ask How to Add Value	How can I enhance my perceived strengths?
	How can I eliminate my perceived weaknesses and turn them into strengths?
	What new attributes can I add to steal a march over the competition?

Paranoia helps you to tackle your task with real vigor. It did not avert Gates's near-fatal reluctance to see the overwhelming importance of the Internet. Gates had huge financial and technological resources to help him recover. You do not. Leaving well enough alone, although tempting, may not be good enough at all. It is a far riskier policy than making intelligent changes.

Taking risks

One of the greatest fears is of taking risks. Logically, there is only one risk: that of being wrong. You can make mistakes in:

- Calculating the value of an idea
- Planning how to exploit the idea
- Implementing the plans

These risks can never be eliminated. But you must be sure that fear of risk is not a cover for lack of confidence in your own abilities. Use the fear of competition to overcome the fear of risks, keeping in mind Gates's words: "If you decline to take risks early, you'll decline in the market later."

Healthy paranoia

The principles that apply to corporations are just as important for Myself Inc. You need a healthy paranoia that does not impair confidence, but keeps you on your toes. See any competition you face as potentially formidable and use the threat to motivate you to improve. Take very seriously the perceptions of your customers – and work relentlessly to shift those perceptions in your favor.

3 Owning the customer

Gates ensured that IBM PCs came only with the Microsoft operating system, which meant that all IBM-compatible PCs also had to use MS-DOS. The PC customer had no choice but to "buy" Microsoft's product. Like Gates, strive to bind the customer to you as closely as possible to establish unique market strength and secure your future.

Set the standard

It is unlikely that you have or could create a built-in position of such power as Microsoft's. Still seek to ensure that your product is so good that customers can see no reason to buy anyone else's. Gates would never have succeeded if Microsoft's products had been markedly inferior to those of the competition. MS-DOS was good enough to deter purchasers from demanding something else.

You need to give the customer reasons to buy only from you even when there are plenty of options. Gates's object was to make Microsoft the industry leader by:

■ Offering the best products
■ Making its products the most useful
■ Keeping prices below the competition.

Do not take "best," "most useful," and "below the competition" for granted. You can be very wrong on all three counts unless you regularly complete the "ask your customers" exercise on page 88 and, most important, then act on any competitive weaknesses.

BILL GATES

Creating Captive Customers

Getting your "business model" right is vital. That means not only the right relationship between costs and prices but the right route to retaining customers.

King C. Gillette had dozens of rivals for the safety razor market. Although safety razors had advantages over the cutthroat, they cost $5 – five times a day's wage. The Gillette product was more expensive to make than others, but no better. All the same, Gillette swept the market. He sold the razor far below cost, but designed it so that only his patented blades could be used. He sold these at a 400 percent mark-up. But customers happily paid five cents a blade because, with six or seven uses, each shave cost only a cent, which compared well with the 10 cents charged by barbers. Gillette had created captive customers by pricing shaves, not razors.

Analyze the market

You cannot sustain a dominant position in the marketplace with your product or service without having first analyzed carefully your customers and competitors. Find out more about customers – their perceptions and demands – by asking four more questions:

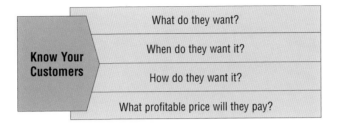

Know Your Customers	What do they want?
	When do they want it?
	How do they want it?
	What profitable price will they pay?

Provide value

Keep checking that you are meeting the demands of your customers. Microsoft overcomes the last hurdle – giving customers an acceptable yet profitable price – by "bundling" much of its software into the PC package. Customers are therefore unaware of the price.

In most cases, that is an impossible ideal. But it is in your interest to keep price out of the decision to buy. If customers have strong enough reasons for buying your products, they will be relatively indifferent to price – so making your life much easier.

Build on your assets

Think of the customer as your greatest asset – then think how to build on that asset. Gates did so by adding hugely profitable applications (such as Word and Powerpoint) to MS-DOS. To see where you can build, draw a square and complete the following customer/product matrix:

- ■ Enter existing customers along the top line.
- ■ Put existing products down the left side.
- ■ Mark off which customers take which products.

How can you fill in the blanks? Your first aim is to sell more existing products to existing customers. New products and new customers are vital, but harder to win, and they take longer to make a profit. Learn from Microsoft, which sometimes failed existing customers but made golden profits by correcting that failure.

5

Turning vision into value

Focusing vision on what you know and understand for maximum effectiveness ● **How Gates got the Internet wrong – and then got it right** ● Chasing "big, hairy audacious goals" to achieve market leadership ● **Backing up vision with the necessary resources, capability, and energy to succeed** ● Learning from making mistakes – and admitting that you made them ● **Developing the right subordinate visions by turning to the customer** ● Viewing Microsoft as "always kind of an underdog thing"

Gates regards vision as opportunity. His intuitive belief that personal computing was the future was certainly visionary. But, as he points out, "vision is free. And it's therefore not a competitive advantage in any way, shape, or form." Unless your vision translates into a marketable product or service, it has no value. If your central vision is tightly focused on what you know and understand, you can develop enough momentum to correct your inevitable misreadings of a fast-moving future.

The core of Bill Gates's thought is an intense belief that the future is progress. In his philosophy, the meaning of human life, society, the economy, technology, and business lies in sustained, vigorous, forward movement. He applies this credo strongly to his business. He expects the technology to become obsolete and to be replaced. He expects the business to mutate as it grows. He believes that change is inherent in all organisms, and that the great manager and the great business proactively turn change to their advantage.

Poor predictive powers

Vision is not prediction. Gates is a prime proof of the dictum of Alan Kay, one of the great intellectual fathers of the PC, that "the best way to predict the future is to invent it." Gates made the future happen by the commercial acumen and drive he brought to the technology solutions that suited his interests. His predictive powers, however, have often failed him, most notably over the all-encompassing future of the Internet.

Gates received criticism amounting to ridicule for the omission of the Internet from the first edition of *The Road Ahead*. He was apparently blind to the fact that the information highway led through the Internet. The book was published in 1995. In the previous spring, according to Gates, Microsoft was betting that the Internet would be "important some day…. But we didn't expect that within two years the Internet would captivate the whole industry and the public's imagination…. Seemingly overnight people by the millions went on to the Internet."

By 1996, when the second edition of the book was published, it was "no exaggeration to say that virtually everything Microsoft does these days is focused in one way or another on the Internet." This astonishing turnabout explains much about "vision" (one of the most used and over-used words in modern management) and much about Gates himself. In *Business the Bill Gates Way* (1999), Des Dearlove writes that Gates regards himself as "an expert in unraveling the technological past from the technological future." His "talent is for understanding what's just around the corner."

That description is wholly contradicted by the Internet story, when the technological future and what was actually happening, let alone just around the corner, eluded Gates for a significant time. The same episode also contradicts Gates's own philosophy of risk-taking: "You can't look at just the past or current state of the market. You have to also look at where it's likely to go, and where it might go under certain circumstances, and then navigate your company based on your best predictions. To win big, sometimes you have to take big risks."

"The Internet had burst into the public's awareness, and the perception was that Microsoft hadn't been invited to the party…. The Internet signified our doom."
Business @ the Speed of Thought

Focusing on the drawbacks

In putting the Internet on the back burner, Gates was influenced by the drawbacks then prevailing. The technology could not support "video conferencing and high-bandwidth applications such as video-on-demand – to say nothing of the needs for security, privacy, reliability, and convenience." Gates also looked too long at the past: "the years of waiting for online services to catch on had made us conservative in our estimate of how soon significant numbers of people would be using interactive networks."

There were also "irritating deficiencies," which caused complaint. The Internet needed faster modems, cheaper communications switches, more powerful PCs in more places, and "richer content." A true visionary, however, would have ignored these quibbles and concentrated on what the Internet really represented: a universal network. As the prime advocate of networking, Gates should have been better placed to spot this future (and to make it happen). The true visionary would also have been encouraged by precedent.

Looking for patterns in the past

The world had seen a previous example of a promising technology with serious limitations that seemed to restrict its value and market. But the deficiencies did not prevent rapid take-off and, as they were remedied, the market exploded. Gates knew all about this precedent. It was the IBM and IBM-compatible PC market, the expansion of which had made him and Microsoft so rich (see p. 26). Extrapolation of the past into the future can be highly misleading, but looking for patterns in the past can be highly illuminating.

A fresh face for computing
The graphical user interface developed at PARC transformed the early PCs, which were not very user-friendly, requiring skills that were counterintuitive and hard to learn for most people.

As Gates has written: "Ironically, when a technology reaches critical mass its weaknesses and limitations almost become strengths as numerous companies, each trying to stake a claim in what quickly turns into a gold rush, step forward to fix the deficiencies." That analysis is perfectly correct. It follows that the task of the visionary is to spot the build-up to critical mass before it occurs, in order to stake the first claim and mine the richest seam of gold.

Taking big risks

When Gates writes about risk, he implies that Microsoft is just such a visionary organization. He states in *Business @ the Speed of Thought*: "To be a market leader, you have to have what business writer and consultant Jim Collins calls 'big, hairy audacious goals'." Gates counts the foundation of Microsoft as just such a venture – a "big bet." Only in hindsight, he argues, does Microsoft's success look preordained. At the time, "most people scoffed." But any company starting at any time in any industry is embarking on a "hairy audacious" venture. It is only in hindsight, if the venture succeeds, that its founders appear to have had vision.

The real problems arise when success has come, and when the successful market leader is confronted with a new, disruptive technology. "Many industry leaders hesitated to move to new technologies for fear of undercutting the success of their existing technologies," explains Gates. This was the case with IBM. That fear explains why it so underestimated the PC market and thus blinded itself to the consequences of its naïve deal with Bill Gates (see p. 63). As he says, the hesitant leaders "learned a hard lesson." The hardest part of the lesson is that they learned it too late.

Hedging your bets

BILL GATES

Gates says, very rightly, "If you decline to take risks early, you'll decline in the market later." His policy, however, is not so audacious as he suggests. He likes to hedge his bets, covering as wide a range as possible (see p. 53). This is not quite what he says: "If you bet big...only a few of these risks have to succeed to provide for your future." In fact, the initial bet on the Internet was very small, even though by the spring of 1991 "Microsoft was betting that the Internet would be important someday."

Microsoft was ensuring that its software could support the Internet: $100 million was being spent annually on "interactive networks of various kinds," although only part of that was expended on the Net. The figure soared to billions once Gates realized that critical mass had arrived before he was ready for it. "The Internet," he now says, "is in an even stronger position than the PC was 15 years ago." Microsoft's position, however, is not as strong as it was then for a variety of reasons, which include a transient failure of vision.

Turning vision into reality

Vision does not start on the far horizon, or even the middle distance. It begins right under your nose, in the proper understanding of what is going on in the here and now. To repeat, vision to Gates is "not a competitive advantage in any way, shape, or form." It has to be accompanied by the action that will turn the vision into reality. That action, in turn, is impossible unless the company has in place, or can acquire, the necessary resources, capability, and energy. For example, when the PC market started to take off, IBM had resources and capability in abundance, but its understanding was erroneous, its vision defective, and its energy misplaced.

In the Gates philosophy, the concentration of organizational energy on the object at hand is inseparable from vision. What you can do, and actually do, has to match what you must do. Necessity does not extend to blue-sky or far-fetched ventures that will "bet the company": that is, risk total failure in the event of error – even though Gates approvingly quotes Boeing's CEO of 1969–86, Thornton "T." Wilson, who said: "If you want to look at it that you're betting the company, I hope we keep doing it."

Boeing is also one of Gates's chosen examples of excellence in the use of the digital nervous system. The

"You can't just look at the past or current state of the market. You also have to look at where it's likely to go, and where it might go under certain circumstances, and then navigate your company based on your best predictions."
Business @ the Speed of Thought

company was a bad example to pick, however, because of Boeing's record of periodic blundering, not in its bets, but in the execution of its choices. In 1998, the aircraft company plunged into losses after taking orders that could not be met with the extant organization of its production machine. Heads rolled, and massive reforms were put in hand. That does not fit Gates's idea of vision.

Evolution rather than revolution

Whatever his strategic and tactical failures, Gates has always ensured that Microsoft is able to execute the vision. That is partly because the vision is deliberately limited to what can be achieved from the existing base – to evolution, rather than revolution. In 1999 the "current audacious goals" were:

- Make the PC "scale in performance" beyond all existing systems.
- Develop computers that "see, listen, and learn."
- Create software to power the new personal companion devices.

These are quite plainly normal evolutions from Microsoft's existing products and capabilities, in no way representing great, daring jumps into the unknown. It would be strange to the point of absurdity if Gates were not pursuing these avenues, which are not so much "initiatives" (his word) but developments, and far from revolutionary. In fact, products already on the market perform the "see, listen, and learn" functions, while software for handheld computers is well-established: although here Gates faces serious opposition from rivals to his own Windows CE product.

On this evidence, "Microsoft's response to digital convergence, in which all devices will use digital technology to work with one another" is singularly tame. It certainly does not justify Gates's claim that "one fact is clear: we have to take these risks in order to have a long-term future." What risks? The risk of inertia, especially for a company with $19 billion of cash available, would have been far greater. It almost seems as though Gates wants to be seen as possessing precisely the type of vision – far-sighted, imaginative, bold, and quite possibly wrong – which he rejects in both word and practice.

Pragmatic visionary

The pragmatic way in which Gates regards vision is amply illustrated by his admissions of mistakes: "believe me, we know a lot about failures at Microsoft." These failures are product failures, rather than consequences of defective vision. The first Microsoft spreadsheet flopped. So did the first database. So did the OS/2 operating system. Other failures included an office machine product and TV-style Internet shows. But Gates claims that the lessons of much of this failure paid off in later products that were smash hits for Microsoft.

The actual vision exemplified by Gates is a vision of Microsoft and what its place should be in the world of information technology. Gates expressed this vision very simply and very clearly in the early days of Microsoft in his original mission statement: "a computer on every desk and in every home, running Microsoft software." Compared to nearly every other mission statement (including his own revised Vision Version 2), this one has every advantage: short, sharp, to the point, and distinctive. Although Gates later dropped the last three words of his statement, getting a computer in every home and on every desk would, of course, have been meaningless to him unless Microsoft provided the software.

Subordinate visions, or strategies, flow from the overall idea. It followed that, as the profit moved downstream, to the software applications that rested on the operating system, Microsoft had to join the movement. Gates took a *cosa nostra* approach to the industry. The customers were "our thing": Microsoft should achieve the largest possible share of the applications market, emulating its achievement in operating systems. As every customer for an IBM or IBM-compatible PC was *de facto* a Microsoft customer, the vision demanded that Microsoft should seek to supply each and every software need, too.

To find the right direction for these subordinate visions, Microsoft turned to the customer. "In software customers always want more," says Gates. "Our customers are always upping the ante, as they should." The difficulty about following the customer, though, is that the customer often has to be led. Indeed, the great breakthroughs come, not from responding to customer demands, but from anticipating them. You could argue that Gates did exactly that with Windows. Before it appeared, only Apple Mac users could have envisioned it. But too often Microsoft has waited for the

"You have to study what customers say about their problems with your products and stay tuned in to what they want, extrapolating from leading-edge buyers to predict future requirements."
Business @ the Speed of Thought

Surviving through paranoia
Andy Grove, CEO of the microchip company Intel, concurs with Gates that fear of the competition is a major driving force behind the long-term commercial success of any business activity.

message from outside, and the wait has sometimes been too long, enabling others to steal valuable leads.

Nothing in Gates's or Microsoft's history resonates with the same visionary importance as Moore's Law. In 1965, Gordon Moore, the cofounder of Intel, foresaw that the trend line for the improvement in chip performance relative to price would continue. In 1975, having been proved right, Moore pronounced what became his law: that chip capacity would double every 18 months with no increase in cost. This had profound implications for Intel, but Gates and Allen were quick to understand the equal impact on Microsoft.

The greater the power and speed of the computer, the more and more potent the applications that it could use. To exploit this explosive potential, Gates formed a pragmatic vision around factors that included the importance of software as opposed to hardware, the role of compatibility (so that machines and programs could work together), and the need to initiate rather than follow trends.

Driven by fear

The presence of the last is ironic in view of the trend-following habits that Microsoft has usually demonstrated. Those habits in turn are curious, given a fundamental characteristic that Gates shares with his partner in the Wintel (Windows and Intel) quasi-monopoly, Andy Grove, the CEO of Intel. The latter called his 1996 book *Only the Paranoid Survive*. In his view, fear contributes powerfully to vision, just as its opposite, complacency, dulls the sight.

Gates expressed this attitude strikingly in a 1995 *Fortune* joint interview with his cofounder, Paul Allen: "The outside perception and inside perception of Microsoft are so different. The view of Microsoft inside Microsoft is always kind of an underdog thing.... In the early days that underdog, almost paranoid, view was a matter of survivial.... Even though if you look back and see that our sales and profits grew by basically 50 percent a year for all these years, what I really remember is worrying all the time."

Allen endorses this recollection, saying that the partners could always see the "downside," even while working away to explore an upside that still dazzles Gates. "We've been climbing a steep mountain here, and you know there's still lots ahead of us," he says. The balance is all-important. In

Gates's idea of vision, you head for the highest peaks, but in the expectation that you may fall off the mountain at any time. Like any expert climber, therefore, you take every precaution to ensure that you stay firmly on the upward slope. The dangers and threats are immediate: the mountain top is in the distance.

Ideas into action

- Make the future happen by driving the business forward vigorously.

- Concentrate on the potential of new developments, not the drawbacks.

- Never impede progress for fear of undercutting the current business.

- Base vision on proper understanding of what is happening now.

- Take all necessary action to protect the long-term future.

- Keep your vision statement short, sharp, to the point, and distinctive.

- Run scared – always bear in mind the risks and threats.

Making a U-turn and invading the Internet

Bill Gates has tried to play down the full extent of his failure of vision over the Internet. The fact remains, however, that Gates subconsciously wished away the full significance of the Net because it is fully "open."

Anybody can enter the Internet and use any of its services with any computer. You do not need the Windows gateway. Worse still, Microsoft's hold on the applications market, and even the systems market, is threatened by the ability to download other people's software from the Net at low prices – or, in many cases, at no cost at all.

By Gates's own account, Microsoft spent very little money or time between 1991, when it hired an "internetworking specialist," and April 1994. Then Gates took key staff away on a "retreat" to discuss the Net; he also devoted his own "Think Week" to the subject (this is his twice-yearly break "to concentrate on the most difficult technical and business problems facing the company"); and he emailed a strategic U-turn to his staff in which he stated, "we're going to make a major bet on the Internet." As a result, within a year, "every team at Microsoft had defined its Internet charter and begun development."

In May 1995, another Gates email, titled "The Internet Tidal Wave," "summarized our strategic directions and decisions, and announced a corporate reorganization" to fit his new analysis of the Net. "The Internet is the most important single development to come along since the IBM PC was launched in 1981," he now stated. That product had created the Microsoft fortunes: now Gates diverted a massive share of $1.4 billion in research and development spending to defend that wealth. By the end of August 1996, a million users had downloaded free copies of Explorer 3.0, Microsoft's massive riposte to Netscape.

Successful launch

Unlike other Microsoft products, Explorer was a wholly credible alternative to the competition from the start. Its launch was a great example of Gates's tenacity and the responsiveness of the organization. He stresses how employees began his awakening

> **"To get a big company moving fast, especially on a many-headed opportunity like the Internet, you have to have hundreds of people participating and coming up with ideas."** *Business @ the Speed of Thought*

with emails. ("Do people all over my company feel free to send me email because we believe in a flat organization?", he asks, "Or do we have a flat organization because people have always been able to send email to me?") The trickle of emails developed into a flood ("just fantastic") after the Microsoft fightback got under way.

As late as March 1997, however, for all Explorer's huge success in seizing market share from Netscape, the Microsoft camp was still sharply divided on whether Windows could be saved. Gates ended the debate decisively: Microsoft would continue to support and upgrade Windows as the interface between the PC user and the Internet (see p. 81). The final decision will be made by a market which, thanks to the Internet, Microsoft no longer owns outright and cannot control. Thanks to Gates's definitive U-turn, though, Microsoft has won breathing space and a battling chance.

GLOSSARY

BANDWIDTH: In computer terms, the measure of the number of bits that can be moved through a circuit in a second. Gates uses the word to describe people's intellectual capacity.

BASIC: Beginners All-purpose Symbolic Instruction Code is a standard coding method for programming computers.

BIT: The smallest amount of information, represented as binary numbers 0 or 1, that can be manipulated by a computer.

CORPORATE IQ: Term used by Gates to refer to the intelligence, knowledge, and expertise of a company.

DIGITAL NERVOUS SYSTEM (DNS): A term Gates uses to refer to the electronic network binding together a company, its customers, and its suppliers.

DOS: *See* MS-DOS.

GRAPHICAL USER INTERFACE: Image-based operating system, such as Windows or Apple's Macintosh operating system, where the user enters commands by using a mouse to click on images or words, as opposed to a character-based operating system, such as MS-DOS, in which instructions are keyed in, usually in code.

INFORMATION TECHNOLOGY (IT): Any and all types of technologies, from computers to satellites, that can process, store, and transmit information.

INTELLECTUAL CAPITAL: The general and specific knowledge which a company possesses in its staff and its databases, and which is treated as an asset equal or superior to physical assets, such as plant and equipment.

INTERNET: The global network of computers that allows transfer of information between them.

INTERNET BROWSER: The interface between the PC and the World Wide Web. *See* World Wide Web.

JAVA: A universal programming language devised by Sun Microsystems and used for a very wide range of Internet applications.

LEARNING ORGANIZATION: Any organization that mutates and develops to reflect new knowledge and experience.

MAINFRAMES: Large computers, capable of processing vast amounts of information, that are connected to a series of terminals.

MOORE'S LAW: A prediction made in 1965 by Gordon Moore, cofounder of Intel, that the number of components that could fit onto a microprocessor would double yearly at constant prices.

MS-DOS: Microsoft Disk Operating System, the initial operating system used on the first IBM PC, which was launched in 1981.

MULTITASKING: Performing several tasks at once.

OPERATING SYSTEM: The interface between the user and the computer that allows applications to be used. *See* MS-DOS and Windows.

OS/2: The operating system developed jointly by IBM and Microsoft for a new line of IBM PCs.

SOFTWARE: Computer programs, such as Microsoft Word for word processing and Excel for spreadsheets, that enable a computer to perform particular data-processing tasks.

WINDOWS: Microsoft's graphics-based operating system for the PC, which has been updated several times.

WINTEL: A contraction that refers to computers that rely on a combination of a Microsoft Windows operating system and Intel's microprocessors.

WORLD WIDE WEB: Network of files, or Websites, that are linked together over the Internet.

BIBLIOGRAPHY

Like most businessmen, Bill Gates has written relatively little about his life and thought – two books, *The Road Ahead* and *Business @ the Speed of Thought*. But he has spoken at length on many occasions to interviewers at all levels. Gates stories and quotations have been collected in *Bill Gates Speaks* by Janet C. Lowe (1998, John Wiley & Sons, New York).

The magazine *Fortune* has published an interview with Gates and Microsoft cofounder Paul Allen, in which they describe how the partners began and grew the business, and another interview with Gates and Steve Jobs, founder of Apple, in which they discuss the future of computing. A third interview records Gates and multi-billionaire investor Warren Buffett as they talk to a student audience about their careers and views.

The many books on Microsoft are led by Randall E. Stross with *The Microsoft Way* (1996, Addison-Wesley, Longman, Reading MA). The story makes for complex reading, but Stross takes a balanced if critical view. Some other authors are still stronger on the criticism, but much less careful about the balance – witness titles like *Barbarians Led by Bill Gates* by Jennifer Edstrom and Marlin Eller (1998, Henry Holt & Co., New York). Uncritical and unbalanced books also exist, such as *Business the Bill Gates Way* by Des Dearlove (1999, Amacom, New York), which offers "10 Secrets of the World's Richest Business Leader." And then, of course, there's the Web, which abounds in unflattering, unofficial Gates sites. Still, he can hardly complain about that.

WORKS CITED

Bill Gates (1995) *The Road Ahead*, Viking Books, New York.
 – (1996) *The Road Ahead* (revised edition), Viking Books, New York.
 – (1999) *Business @ the Speed of Thought: Using a Digital Nervous System*, Warner Books, New York.
Andrew S. Grove (1996) *Only the Paranoid Survive*, Bantam, Doubleday Dell, New York.
Geoffrey James (1997) *Giant Killers*, Orion, London.
Anthony Sampson (1995) *Company Man: the Rise and Fall of Corporate Life*, HarperCollins, London.
Peter M. Senge (1990) *The Fifth Discipline*, Doubleday, New York.
Alfred P. Sloan (1963) *My Years at General Motors*, Doubleday, New York.
Thomas A. Stewart (1997) *Intellectual Capital: the New Wealth of Organizations*, Doubleday, New York.
Randall E. Stross (1996) *The Microsoft Way: the Real Story of How the Company Outsmarts its Competition*, Addison-Wesley, Longman, Reading MA.

Index

Page numbers in *italics*
refer to picture captions.

INDEX

Robert Heller

Robert Heller is himself a prolific author of management books. The first, *The Naked Manager*, published in 1972, established Heller as an iconoclastic, wide-ranging guide to managerial excellence – and incompetence. Heller has drawn on the extensive knowledge of managers and management he acquired as the founding editor of *Management Today*, Britain's premier business magazine, which he headed for 25 years. Books such as *The Supermanagers*, *The Decision-makers*, *The Superchiefs* and (most recently), *In Search of European Excellence* have all emphasized how to succeed by using the latest ideas on change, quality, and motivation. In 1990 Heller wrote *Culture Shock*, one of the first books to describe how information technology would revolutionize management and business. Since then, as writer, lecturer, and consultant, Heller has continued to tell managers how to "Ride the Revolution." His books for Dorling Kindersley's Essential Managers series are international bestsellers.

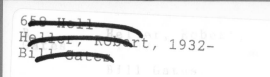

658 Hell
Heller, Robert, 1932-
Bill Gates

DATE